America's Uncounted People

Report of the

ADVISORY COMMITTEE ON PROBLEMS OF CENSUS ENUMERATION
Division of Behavioral Sciences
National Research Council

CAROLE W. PARSONS, *Editor*

NATIONAL ACADEMY OF SCIENCES
WASHINGTON, D.C. 1972

𝒟

NOTICE: The study reported herein was undertaken under the aegis of the National Research Council with the express approval of the Governing Board of the NRC. Such approval indicated that the Board considered that the problem is of national significance; that elucidation of the problem required scientific or technical competence; and that the resources of the NRC were particularly suitable to the conduct of the project. The institutional responsibilities of the Research Council were then discharged in the following manner:

The members of the study committee were selected for their individual scholarly competence and judgment, with due consideration for the balance and breadth of disciplines. Responsibility for all aspects of this report rests with the study committee, to whom our sincere appreciation is expressed.

Although the reports of our study committees are not submitted for approval to the Academy membership nor to the Council, each report is reviewed by a second group of scientists according to procedures established and monitored by the Academy's Report Review Committee. Such reviews are intended to determine, *inter alia,* whether the major questions and relevant points of view have been addressed and whether the reported findings, conclusions, and recommendations arose from the available data and information. Distribution of the report is permitted only after satisfactory completion of this review process.

This document is based on work completed under Contract No. Cco-9336 between the U.S. Department of Commerce, Bureau of the Census, the U.S. Office of Economic Opportunity, and the National Academy of Sciences of May 28, 1969; and Contract No. 81-09-70-17 between the Manpower Administration of the U.S. Department of Labor and the National Academy of Sciences of June 8, 1971.

Available from

Printing and Publishing Office
National Academy of Sciences
2101 Constitution Avenue, N.W.
Washington, D.C. 20418

ISBN 0-309-02026-3
Library of Congress Catalog Card Number 72-76310

Printed in the United States of America

Foreword

The Division of Behavioral Sciences has reason to be pleased with the excellent work of the Advisory Committee on Problems of Census Enumeration. The Committee has provided an informative introduction to the research questions posed by underenumeration in the Census of Population and to the impressive number of attempts that have been made by the Bureau of the Census and a few other government agencies to resolve them. The Committee has also provided an extensive set of new suggestions and ideas that deserve serious consideration.

The value orientation of the Committee should, however, be stressed. When discussing, in Chapter 7, the issue of registration systems and file matching—searching for data pertaining to the same individual in many different record systems—the Committee is turned away by the possibility that such efforts to improve census coverage "might lead to encroachments and harassment for all citizens—not merely the uncounted—although they might bear unequally on different sectors or classes." The Committee suggests that, *prima facie,* the benefit to be obtained from efforts to improve census coverage is not worth more than a very small additional privacy cost.

Yet, one possible interpretation of the Committee's own evidence is that the problem of underenumeration is not ever likely to be solved by continuing to count the entire population at a sequence of widely spaced points in time. Nor are any of the elaborate demographic and other procedures for estimating the extent and geographic location of the census undercount likely to provide adequate information about why people are missed, and from that conclusions about better ways to find them.

If this is true, and if it is crucial to locate some of the missed people, both to correct the counts and to discover why and how they were missed in order to improve census-taking methods, then one might ask whether some device (Social Security numbers perhaps) for counting individuals whenever and wherever they appear in any file may be essential.

Moreover, given such a substantial possible benefit from matching files, have we exaggerated the privacy costs? To count the population, all that would have to be recorded and matched are people's names, ages, sex, race, residence at the time of the census, and Social Security numbers. What invasions of privacy would assembling such limited information from many files produce? Research into other details about those missed by the census might involve looking at other information about them from other files, but the only fact added would be that the individual was not counted in the census. And that could be done for small samples and continued only until the results were clear.

It seems likely that almost everyone appears somewhere at some point during a *period* of time and that the way to obtain a complete count is to combine redundant records of those appearances with an effective system for eliminating duplicates. Faced with the costs of the various, probably inferior, alternatives, and the possibility of great gains with no loss of privacy, are the Committee's value-weights perhaps extreme? Or is the Committee right in foregoing what appears to be a relatively simple technological solution to the underenumeration problem because of its concern about the still unexamined ethical and social consequences of such a solution? These issues, as well as other important research questions identified by the Committee, deserve serious consideration by those who seek to understand the current state and prospects of American society.

JAMES N. MORGAN, *Chairman*
Division of Behavioral Sciences

Preface

The Advisory Committee on Problems of Census Enumeration was established by the National Academy of Sciences in the Division of Behavioral Sciences of the National Research Council in the spring of 1969, in response to a request from the Bureau of the Census for advice on ways to improve the completeness and accuracy of information collected in the decennial censuses of population and in intercensal household surveys conducted by the Bureau or by other government agencies. The problems and issues involved in this advisory undertaking were explored by a six-member *ad hoc* group— Philip Converse, Albert Biderman, Morris Hansen, Niles Hansen, S. M. Miller, and Lee Rainwater—and members of the Census Bureau staff convened by the Division late in January 1969. That meeting pointed to the desirability of having the proposed advisory activity co-sponsored by other federal agencies that are major users of census and census-related statistics. More important, it concluded that the problem of census underenumeration should be perceived as the central, but not the exclusive, concern of a broadly conceived long-range program of research on census-taking problems.

Two agencies, the Office of Economic Opportunity and the Manpower Administration of the Department of Labor, joined the Census Bureau in supporting the Advisory Committee. The work of the Committee has centered upon five separate but interrelated tasks:

- Considering how the social costs associated with under-enumeration might best be estimated, along with the social benefits that might accrue from remedying coverage deficiencies

- Reviewing the state of knowledge about social conditions and attitudes that bear on the ability of government agencies to collect complete and accurate information from all elements of the population
- Providing advice on research and experimental efforts leading to a better understanding of the reasons for incomplete coverage in the Census of Population and in current surveys
- Recommending measures and procedures that appear likely to reduce or mitigate current deficiencies in coverage
- Designing a continuing research program directed toward the measurement and reduction of underenumeration in current surveys and subsequent censuses of population

These tasks were addressed in several stages. When the Committee met for the first time, in June 1969, the 1970 Censuses of Population and Housing were still almost a year in the future. Hence, in its *Interim Report,* completed in the fall of 1969, the Committee suggested ways in which the 1970 Census field operations might be used experimentally to learn more about the reasons for incomplete coverage or inaccurate reporting in a full-scale census. For example, the Committee encouraged the Census Bureau's already evident interest in urban ethnography as a method for developing new hypotheses about the causes of observed deficiencies in censuses and social surveys. It proposed further studies of the effects of census public information campaigns, and of the advantages to be gained from using simplified census questionnaires. It recommended that the Bureau continue to examine the process of delivering census forms by mail, and urged that tests be made of the ability of community organizations to conduct censuses and surveys in hard-to-enumerate areas.

In May 1971, the Committee submitted its *Final Report* to the sponsoring agencies. In that document, the themes of the *Interim Report* were developed more fully and additional possibilities, such as alternative census-taking procedures and classification frameworks were examined. More important, the recommendations in the *Final Report* were not limited to research opportunities suggested by established enumeration practices, but they extended to a continuing program of studies that should lead to improvements in the ability of government agencies to collect complete and accurate information about the size and characteristics of the nation's population.

The present text is essentially an edited version of the *Final Report.* It differs from the original document in the serial organization of chapters and in the arrangement of some material within chapters. In style of argument, and particularly in the phrasing of specific recommendations, it also addresses a broader readership than the staffs of the three sponsoring agencies.

The recommendations in the report flow from two principal concerns of the Advisory Committee: the need for increased effort to understand the social and behavioral aspects of census and survey operations; and the corresponding need for better measures of the importance to users of deficiencies in the counts, and in measures of the characteristics, of specific population subgroups. The recommendations are, moreover, cast in the form of strategic approaches to research that create opportunities for social data producers and users alike to engage in cooperative efforts to improve the overall quality of census and census-related statistics.

In the course of performing its several tasks, the Advisory Committee was able to draw on the knowledge and experience of a large number of social scientists who participated in the work of its seven subcommittees. Their names and the subcommittees on which they served are listed in Appendix D. The Committee is exceptionally grateful to its subcommittee members, whose contributions helped to produce a report of far greater scope and detail than would otherwise have been possible. Also, the Advisory Committee would like to express special appreciation to Carole Parsons, the Committee's Executive Secretary. She was indispensable in enabling the group to perform its tasks, and she played a critical role in drafting and editing both this document and the earlier interim and final reports. For her, our admiration is enormous and our gratitude profound.

The Advisory Committee wishes to acknowledge the assistance given by staff and members of the Division of Behavioral Sciences. Henry David, the Division's Executive Secretary, was an invaluable source of constructive advice throughout the Committee's deliberations. Alexander Clark, the Committee's first Executive Secretary, organized and guided early Committee and subcommittee activities, and later, as Acting Executive Secretary of the Division, continued to offer the Committee encouragement and assistance. The Division's Chairman, James N. Morgan, and two other members of the Division's Executive Committee, Robert McCormick Adams and Philip Converse, were constructive critics of an early draft. Kingsley Davis, Paul Demeny, Philip Hauser, Sar Levitan, and Charles Willie, who served as independent reviewers of the document, made helpful suggestions. The assistance generously offered by Robert R. Hume, Publications Editor of the National Academy of Sciences, was gratefully accepted.

Full recognition and appreciation should also be given to those representatives of the three sponsoring agencies, and of other interested federal departments and bureaus, who made special efforts to assure that the Committee was adequately informed of current thinking and research on problems of census data collection and use. In particular, the Committee wishes to thank Benjamin Tepping, Conrad Taeuber, Joseph Daly, Jacob Siegel, and Meyer Zitter of the Census Bureau staff; Thomas Tomlinson of the Office of Economic Opportunity; and Stuart Garfinkle of the Manpower Administration of the Department of Labor. Welcome assistance in understanding the uses of census data in policy making and in program planning and administration was provided on several occasions by Harold Guthrie, David Lane, Bette Mahoney, and Gordon Sutton of the Office of Economic Opportunity; Norman Root of the Department of Labor; Ezra Glazer, Bryan Mitchell, Richard Simonson, and Morris Ullman of the Department of Health, Education, and Welfare; Richard Grant of the Department of Agriculture; and Roye Lowry and Margaret Martin of the Office of Management and Budget.

There are, in addition, many unnamed individuals in the sponsoring agencies, or on the staffs of other federal and state agencies, who have made informal contributions to the Committee's work, either through conversations with staff or by providing copies of relevant published material. To them, the Committee is in debt.

Throughout its two-year tenure, the Committee has been fortunate to have had at various times the willing and efficient secretarial assistance of Mrs. Susan Jobst, Miss Ann Garrigan, Miss Sally Hillsgrove, and Mrs. Anne Baker Moss. The Committee, however, wishes to express special thanks to Mrs. Lindsay Spooner for the many hours she spent typing and retyping more drafts of the manuscript than she probably cares to remember.

Although this report was prepared for the Bureau of the Census of the Department of Commerce, the Office of Economic Opportunity, and the Manpower Administration of the Department of Labor, it does not represent the offical opinion or policy of any of the sponsoring agencies. The Committee is also solely responsible for the factual accuracy of all material contained in the report, as well as for opinions attributed to the three agencies.

It would be unusual, indeed, to find that a document with more than a dozen authors carries the full concurrence of each. This report, perhaps more than others, is the product of a Committee whose members frequently addressed important issues and problems from different substantive perspectives. Hence, although the report has the endorsement of the full Committee, no one member should be or would want to be held responsible for every detail or point of view expressed.

S. M. MILLER, *Chairman*
Advisory Committee on
Problems of Census Enumeration

Advisory Committee on Problems
of Census Enumeration

xi

Contents

xiii

Introduction

Social statistics are quantitative statements about the composition and structure of a society. In the United States, since the earliest days of the republic, statistical information about the size, distribution, and social characteristics of the nation's citizenry has served to legitimate and to guide public decision making. Article I, Section 2, of the Constitution stipulates that the government of the United States shall be representative and that a Census of Population shall be conducted at regular intervals. The Census Act of 1790 further directed that the first official count of persons present within the borders of the new nation should include information on the usual residence, age, sex, race, and free or indentured status of enumerated persons.[1]

Two centuries of national growth and societal transformation have greatly expanded the functions of government and, with them, the scope and uses of social statistics. Instead of one census, intended primarily for apportioning political representation, there are now more than seven.[2] Instead of a few large-scale, comprehensive enumerations at widely spaced intervals, there are today, in addition to the decennial censuses, several complementary systems of statistical reporting. Most notable is the Current Population Survey (CPS), a rotating sample of approximately 50,000 households, which provides monthly information on labor force characteristics and, at less fre-

[1] For an overview of the conduct and content of the early censuses, see Hyman Alterman, *Counting People: The Census in History* (New York: Harcourt, Brace & World), 1969.
[2] The seven major ones are the Censuses of Population, Housing, Agriculture, Business, Manufactures, Governments, and Transportation.

1

quent intervals, statistics on a broad range of other subjects. There is also a small but continuing household health survey and a variety of administrative sources from which statistical information about the society is regularly derived. For example, social statistics are produced in the process of collecting federal income taxes, in administering the Social Security system, and as by-products of government programs addressed to a multitude of more or less specific social and economic needs.

More striking still is the variety of uses that social statistics now serve. Counts of the number and characteristics of resident persons continue to be the basis for apportioning legislatures and for allocating votes within the Electoral College. Yet, today, the importance of social statistics is also measured in terms of the information they provide about the nature of major societal problems, the resources available for addressing them, and the consequences of government programs designed to achieve specified policy objectives.

This report is primarily concerned with one major segment of the vast social data-gathering activities of the federal government—the Census of Population—and with one specific census problem—the failure to enumerate an estimated 3 percent[3] of the nation's population in recent decennial censuses. However, in examining the census undercount phenomenon, it soon became apparent that because of the size and complexity of the national social data-gathering enterprise, underenumeration in the population census cannot be neatly separated from other problems, both statistical and social, that affect

[3] The 3 percent should be treated as an estimate that requires additional validation. Although widely used and accepted, it may be subject to a substantial range of error. The principal method from which the estimate is derived (demographic analysis, discussed below on pp. 26–28 and 101–103) makes a number of assumptions that merit further study. The following facts point to at least one reason for further questioning: Each of the population censuses from 1940 to 1960 produced national population estimates for subsequent census dates, after taking account of births, deaths, immigration, and emigration, that closely agreed with the actual counts shown by each subsequent census, thereby implying approximately equal amounts of net underenumeration in each successive census. Yet, during that twenty-year period, major changes were made in census enumeration procedures, and there were, perhaps, also important changes in the social circumstances of the population. Consistency under such varying conditions cannot help but raise questions. The 3 percent national estimate is, however, generally accepted, and the Advisory Committee will proceed on the assumption that it roughly approximates the magnitude of underenumeration in national census totals.

the society's ability to compile an accurate, comprehensive portrait of its structure and membership.

The crux of recent concern about census underenumeration is not the simple 3 percent shortfall in *national census totals* so much as the larger deficiencies in the *counts of specific population subgroups,* most notably young black men.[4] From a statistical perspective, the existence of differential undercounting means that coverage deficiencies, like other, perhaps related, data weaknesses (misclassification errors being the most prominent example) may seriously undermine the quality and hence, the practical utility of official social data series. From the point of view of some of the major social issues of recent years, however, census undercounting[5] raises equally important questions about the ways in which American society functions so as to deny particular groups representation in its official data series.

At a time when political institutions, from small community organizations to large federal bureaucracies, are being asked to assume greater responsibility for initiating and directing change in the structure, purposes, and quality of American life, knowledge that underenumeration occurs unevenly invites queries about the social conditions associated with incomplete census counts. To what extent, for example, are such conditions created or reinforced, albeit inadvertently, by public action based on inaccurate or incomplete statistical information? To what extent do uncounted persons prefer not to become "socially visible" in a census? Does their preference for anonymity perhaps indicate profound estrangement from the values and everyday life experiences of the counted majority?

Questions such as these led to establishment of the Advisory Committee on Problems of Census Enumeration. The three Committee sponsors—the Bureau of the Census, the Office of Economic Opportunity, and the Manpower Administration of the Department

---

[4] Concern with census undercount of blacks is not new. Throughout much of the 19th century, analysts questioned the accuracy of the decennial enumerations of Negroes. For a review of such criticisms see: Reynolds Farley, *Growth of the Black Population* (Chicago: Markham), 1970, especially pp. 23–26.

[5] Although the terms are sometimes used interchangeably in this report, it should be noted that in its precise technical usage, *net underenumeration* denotes the difference between the actual size of the resident population of an area and the population counted within its borders by an official census. *Net undercounts,* in contrast, are compounded of net underenumeration and misclassification errors, such as faulty reporting of age.

of Labor—share a common interest in complete, accurate information about the characteristic features of American society, as well as in understanding the contexts and consequences of social data generation and use. The Bureau of the Census, for its part, has worked long and hard to assure the accuracy of census statistics, but in its studies of underenumeration has thus far been unable to move with confidence beyond the point of estimating the extent and principal components of national census undercoverage. Development of a methodology for evaluating the *overall completeness* of the decennial censuses has been one of the Bureau's major preoccupations and achievements during the past two decades. Yet, as the Bureau readily acknowledges, an estimation method that does not provide information about where *differential undercounting* occurs locally is not of great help to major users of the census, such as the Advisory Committee's two other sponsors, who require accurate, comparable, small-area statistics of the sort uniquely collected in the decennial enumerations. It is helpful to know that black men are the most undercounted group in American society, generally, but it is also important to know where uncounted blacks can be found, what their distinguishing characteristics are, and whether uncounted whites, who constitute an even larger group in absolute numbers, might share all the characteristics, except race, that are hypothesized[6] for uncounted blacks—namely, inadequate education, unemployment, and effective disenfranchisement.

The following chapters represent an effort to identify systematically the many research questions posed by underenumeration in the census and other large-scale social data-gathering activities. In Chapter 1, an inquiry is made into the effects of differential undercounting on the multiple uses to which census data are put. In Chapter 2, existing information and leading hypotheses about the demographic and social characteristics of uncounted persons are presented and discussed. In Chapter 3, the Census Research and Evaluation Programs are examined, and ways in which they might draw more fully

---

[6] See Leon Pritzker and N. D. Rothwell, "Procedural Difficulties in Taking Past Censuses in Predominantly Negro, Puerto Rican, and Mexican Areas," in David M. Heer (Ed.), *Social Statistics and the City* (Cambridge, Massachusetts: Harvard University Press for the Joint Center for Urban Studies of the Massachusetts Institute of Technology and Harvard University), 1968, p. 71; and Earle J. Gerson, "Methodological and Interviewing Problems in Household Surveys of Employment Problems in Urban Poverty Neighborhoods," *Proceedings of the Social Statistics Section of the American Statistical Association*, 1969, p. 22.

on a larger range of potentially useful social science knowledge and research experience are suggested. Chapter 3 responds, in other words, to the Committee's central recommendation, that *the present conception of enumeration-related research should be expanded in ways that place greater stress on the relationship between census-taking problems, such as underenumeration, and the social contexts in which censuses and surveys are conducted.*

Chapter 4 outlines the principal features of such an expanded research perspective. It considers the research implications of conceiving the census as a socially organized activity interposed among other socially organized activities that to varying degrees enhance or reduce the possibility of achieving an accurate count. Chapters 5 and 6 contain specific research recommendations. In the former, projects that build upon relatively well-charted lines of enumeration-related inquiry are proposed, along with longer-term exploratory studies using research methods not customarily employed in the Census Research and Evaluation Programs. In the latter, examples are offered of analytic approaches that should be examined as part of the continuing effort to improve the quality of population statistics for small geographic areas.

Finally, in Chapter 7, attention is given to the organizational requirements of a research program in which major users of census statistics would find opportunities for active participation and support. A central argument of the chapter, as well as of many earlier sections of the report, is that if social data collection and use problems are indeed related to other problems of societal concern today, then institutions and groups responsible for counting America's people, and institutions and groups responsible for serving their needs, clearly have large areas of mutual research interest.

1   The Importance of Census Accuracy: Implications for Statistical and Social Policy

How, how much, and to whom does it matter that there is a census undercount, that it may be large in some places, and that it seems to involve some categories of the population more than others? The search for answers to such questions leads directly to consideration of the varied purposes for which census statistics are collected and analyzed.

Census data are used, first of all, to apportion political representation at many levels of American government. However, in addition to the several political dimensions of census data collection and interpretation, on which turn important questions of equitable apportionment and minority participation, census statistics also serve as guides in the process of formulating public policy. By drawing attention to quantifiable dimensions of collective human behavior, they help to organize analysis and understanding of public policy issues. By describing features of the social system in quantitative terms, they encourage anticipatory analysis of the consequences of competing policy recommendations. Social statistics of the sort collected in the census do not dictate the substance of policy, but they can lessen the chance that misinformed or impressionistic judgments will lead to costly errors in social policy design.

Census statistics are also among the tools used in translating legislative mandates into working social programs. They help to define universes of need, to identify areas with special problem characteristics, and to distribute program funds among administrative jurisdictions. To these significant public policy uses, moreover, one must add the commercial uses of the census in planning, forecasting, and market research, as well as the many less direct research uses that cumulatively serve fundamental knowledge needs of the society.

Not until the advent of the social welfare legislation of the 1960's did census statistics for small areas (counties, cities, tracts, and neighborhoods) acquire such ubiquitous importance. One need only look at the census data requirements created by federal statute during the last decade to see that there has been a quantitative change in the number and variety of uses to which census data for small areas are now put.[1] Concurrently, state and local governments have also come to rely increasingly on local-area census counts for allocating tax revenues among their subordinate jurisdictions, for program planning and forecasting, for locating transportation facilities, hospitals, and schools, and for justifying their eligibility for various categories of federal financial assistance.

Earlier in the nation's history, most major social policy initiatives were served by highly imperfect indicators of the condition and needs of large segments of the society. Indeed, the economic depression of the 1930's can be seen as a watershed in the history of federal social data collection and use, for it was in 1937 that the Congress, recognizing the need for better labor force information, appropriated funds for the first nationwide census of unemployment. Now, twenty-five years later, the situation is even more changed. From a focus on national unemployment rates, attention is today shifting to concern about pockets of chronic joblessness. Together with massive public investments in higher education, there is an effort to provide remedial instruction for specific categories of children and adults who would otherwise be unable to take even ordinary advantage of standard educational opportunities. There are programs to distribute surplus food to the urban poor, to provide bilingual instruction to children of Spanish-speaking families, to rebuild blighted central cities, to discourage migration from rural areas, to support community health centers, and to encourage citizens to participate in the planning and implementation of government-financed efforts to improve the quality of their own daily lives. All these specifically targeted efforts, as well as many others, are perforce dependent at some point on statistical profiles of small

---

[1] A broad, if unsystematic, survey of the uses of small-area census statistics will be found in U.S. Congress, House of Representatives, Subcommittee on Census and Statistics of the Committee on Post Office and Civil Service, *Hearings on the 1970 Census and Legislation Related Thereto*, 91st Congress, 1st Session (Washington, D.C.: U.S. Government Printing Office), April–June 1969, especially Part I, pp. 1–80 and 343–435.

fractions of the population that tend to be unevenly distributed geographically and that are frequently describable in terms of employment insecurity, educational disadvantage, and other kinds of deprivation.

New requirements for accurate, precise, area-specific social statistics have, moreover, been reinforced by refinements in the style of administering social programs. At the federal level, future historians will very likely point to institutionalization of the planning and evaluation functions in government as one of the more significant contributions of the poverty programs of the 1960's. However, the Appalachian Redevelopment Act, the Economic Opportunity Act, the Housing and Urban Development Act, civil rights legislation, and a variety of other health, welfare, education, and labor programs also make eligibility for federal assistance contingent on submission of planning and evaluation documents by state and municipal governments.

Recognition of these varied uses of census and other social statistics throws into bolder relief recent controversy about the Census of Population. On one hand, there is greater confidence than ever before in the skill with which the federal government conducts the decennial enumerations. On the other, there appears to be growing doubt about the effectiveness of conventional census-taking procedures, however skillfully applied, and thus about the reliability of the census totals they produce. This contradiction reflects the different perspectives from which the Census of Population is regarded by its producers, its users, and the groups directly affected by the data it generates.

The Census Bureau, for example, is concerned about the *accuracy* of the statistics—about the verity of the portrait of American society that census data provide. Other federal and state agencies that use census statistics are primarily concerned with the degree of *administrative efficiency* that such data help to make possible. Their tasks, which often involve allocation or redistribution of money and services, will be better served to the extent that census data can provide at least some hints about undercounted population subgroups, even though the groups in question are not described with the degree of confidence that the Census Bureau would prefer.

Finally, there are groups within the society that are concerned that their presence and needs receive clearer *recognition.* Often they are groups that until recently have been denied full membership in the society and that thus demand special efforts to assure that their voices are heard and their numbers noted. They are not impressed by arguments that government data collection operations normally cannot be designed so as to achieve perfect accuracy or coverage, or that even relatively large margins of error can often be shown to have little effect on the formation of policy or the administration of programs.

The Putative Effects of Census Errors

Errors in the Census of Population are generally considered to have three kinds of adverse consequences for public policy design and administration. First, substantial *inequities* are believed to occur when decisions affecting specific geographic areas turn upon deficiencies in coverage of the number of persons resident in those areas. Legislative apportionment and federal and state grant-in-aid decisions are the most frequently mentioned cases. Second, unless it can be assumed that the census characteristics of uncounted persons are distributed in the same way as those of counted persons in demographic strata with large undercounts, there may be significant *distortions* in the social data used to define needs for many programs in education, housing, health, and manpower.[2] If the undercount in an area happens to vary systematically with the incidence of poverty or illiteracy, both the size and the needs of the populations to which welfare and education programs are addressed could be seriously underestimated.

Moreover, even if counted and uncounted persons prove to have similar census characteristics, uncounted persons might still have other distinguishing features, such as unusual patterns of family life, that would, if known, affect the design and administration of special social services. Thus, the failure to count some people in a census could be viewed as a symptom of some social problem or of anomalous social circumstances that cannot be adequately understood until the missing individuals are found and their life circumstances fully described.

Third, census errors matter because the census is central to a large network of complementary data collection activities and correlative statistical series. Census counts and data on population characteristics

[2] For a discussion of two hypotheses about the effect of underenumeration on labor force statistics, see Denis F. Johnston and James R. Wetzel, "Effect of the Census Undercount on Labor Force Estimates," *Monthly Labor Review*, 92, March 1969, pp. 3–13.

are used as reference points in the interpretation of social statistics collected by the government in many other household and institutional surveys. They serve as bench marks in the construction of practically every official time series dealing with population characteristics and are the basis for most intercensal estimates of population change. In particular, data collected in the Current Population Survey (CPS)—the principal source of continuous statistical series on such topics as labor force participation, marital status, family income, ethnicity, and migration—are adjusted monthly to agree with population figures projected forward from the most recent decennial census. Intercensal population estimates for states, metropolitan areas, and counties are regularly developed using methods that employ census counts in combination with current statistics on births, deaths, migration, school enrollments, sales tax collections, and passenger-vehicle registrations.[3] Since there are some grounds for the belief that the problem of underenumeration is at least as large in the CPS as it is in the census (one out of four young adult nonwhite males is thought to be unrepresented in the CPS sample),[4] and since census undercoverage affects decennial population totals for states and smaller geographic subunits to an unknown extent, underenumeration may produce substantial *cumulative errors* in all the official data series, estimates, and projections that in any way employ the census as a principal point of departure.[5]

Finally, inaccurate or incomplete census statistics may have important implications for private decision making and research. Market survey findings and local labor force estimates on which many commercial activities depend could be misleading to the degree that disproportionately large undercounts occur in certain areas. Scientific analysis of the structural features of major social institutions,

---

[3] For a description of the methods used, see U.S. Bureau of the Census, *Current Population Reports,* Series P-26, "Federal-State Cooperative Program for Population Estimates," and *Current Population Reports,* Series P-25, No. 427 and 436.

[4] Jacob S. Siegel, "Completeness of Coverage of Nonwhite Population in the 1960 Census and Current Estimates, and Some Implications," in David M. Heer (Ed.), *Social Statistics and the City* (Cambridge, Massachusetts: Harvard University Press for the Joint Center for Urban Studies of the Massachusetts Institute of Technology and Harvard University), 1968, p. 31.

[5] The effects may be compounded by problems peculiar to other series. For example, see Mitsuo Ono and Herman P. Miller, "Income Nonresponses in the Current Population Survey," *Proceedings of the Social Statistics Section of the American Statistical Association,* 1969, pp. 277–288.

and of the dynamics of social change, could be affected by flaws in basic social data on family composition, migration flows, economic opportunities, and stratification patterns.[6] Indeed, independently conducted social surveys could be affected not only by errors in the data used to develop sampling frames, but also by the extent to which census undercoverage and related deficiencies are linked to patterns of behavior characteristically found among certain sub-classes of the population. Census enumeration procedures and the interviewing methods of most household surveys are similar. Hence, aspects of interviewer and respondent behavior that impinge upon census completeness and accuracy very likely diminish the quality of social data collected by wholly autonomous survey operations.

Tolerable Margins of Error in Population Statistics

Despite the many suspected consequences of census errors, attempts to develop measures of their actual cost and of the benefits to be de-rived from reducing them have not been notably successful. One rea-son is that there is disagreement about the most appropriate purposes of census data collection. Some argue that the policy and research needs for statistical information have become so varied, so detailed, and so precise as to move the required level of census accuracy close to perfection.[7] Others maintain that "the census should be viewed primarily as the means of selecting areas for further study rather than as the source for all the data that may be needed. . . ."[8] Given this lack of an agreed measure of the shortcomings of present census sta-tistics, it is hard to assign a cost to data deficiencies or to determine the amount of investment that should be made in order to reduce them.

A second difficulty arises from the fact that losses due to census inadequacies frequently cannot be expressed in dollars and cents. Some, such as formula-grant misallocations, may be amenable to conventional pricing, but other moral and social costs cannot be ex-pressed in monetary terms. By being counted and described in a census, individuals are grouped in ways that make them "socially visible." They acquire an identity in terms of the society's most

[6] See Donald J. Bogue, "The Pros and Cons of Self-Enumeration," *Demo-graphy*, 2, 1965, pp. 601–606.
[7] *Ibid.*, p. 602.
[8] Conrad Taeuber and Morris H. Hansen, "Self Enumeration as a Census Method," *Demography*, 3, 1966, p. 292.

common organizational and cultural arrangements, gaining therein enhanced opportunity to participate in the distribution of a range of societal rewards and responsibilities. The census, in effect, increases both the visibility and the legitimacy of individual claims on the rights, privileges, and obligations of societal membership. To the extent that some groups are less fully counted than others, however, the (presumed) asset of social visibility becomes, like other participatory opportunities, unequally shared, and persons who have characteristics in common with uncounted persons are denied full symbolic recognition of their membership in American society.

One illustration is the use of the 1970 Census to apportion the Congress and the 50 state legislatures in accordance with judicially prescribed principles of arithmetic equity. Given the size of most congressional constituencies, it seems doubtful that local under-enumeration would affect the national apportionment pattern. State legislative districts, however, could be significantly affected, since they are usually smaller. Moreover, at least in theory, the combined effect of census undercounting and the "one man, one vote" requirement is to increase the possibility of relative denial of congressional and state representation. Not everyone located in the same district, counted or not, is equally penalized, but groups, whether defined in terms of geography, race, sex, age, or other characteristics, do suffer.

A third impediment to successful measurement of the cost of counting errors stems from the pervasive but often incalculable influence of the census and census-related statistical series on a large and disparate array of societal activities. For example, it has been roughly estimated that every uncounted resident of New York City might represent a loss to the municipal government of $35 per year in state aid.[9] Yet it is not at all clear how similar cost–benefit measures can be assigned to errors in bodies of statistics that serve the planning, evaluation, and day-to-day information needs of different units of government or of decision making characteristically performed in the private sector.

In recent years, numerous planning efforts in federal agencies and the Congress have sought to assess the need for specialized social services on the basis of census or Current Population Survey data that provide measures of such variables as the economic status of persons recently migrated from rural areas to cities (as, for example, in the case of manpower training legislation). Others have required

[9] *The New York Times*, August 25, 1970.

estimates of the size of such population subgroups as employable adult women (day care centers), persons over 65 (Medicare),[10] children with limited English-speaking ability (bilingual education), and children aged 5 to 17 in families with income of less than $3,000 per year (compensatory education). In addition, there are many programs—Community Action (administered by the Office of Economic Opportunity), Adult Basic Education (Department of Health, Education, and Welfare), and Model Cities (Department of Housing and Urban Development)—that require communities and states to justify their applications for federal support with detailed statistical portraits of relevant local conditions or with carefully drawn plans for the expenditure of federal money, once awarded. Still other state, municipal, and private planning activities depend heavily on census data that help them to define universes of need, to establish program priorities, and to disburse appropriations.

Theoretically, the utility of the statistical information employed in such activities might be estimated in terms of the expected value of the consequences of all decisions the information affects, less the expected value of the consequences of the same decisions were the information either not available or less accurate and complete. In the day-to-day operation of government programs, however, as well as in private decision making, it is hard to pinpoint every turn at which statistics could be said to shape or to determine the final outcome of any single policy or program decision, and it is virtually impossible to assign costs and gains to the social consequences of those outcomes.

How is a quantified value to be assigned to corroborative information that serves primarily to reassure a decision maker because it agrees with other facts at his disposal? What cost should be attributed to deficiencies in official statistical series that encourage unwarranted public optimism about the improving status of certain minority groups or that provoke charges of inequity in the implementation of proposed federal–state revenue-sharing schemes? Indeed, since the success or failure of current efforts to devolve administrative responsibilities from federal to local units of government will no doubt be judged partly according to the competence and fairness with which

---

[10] Former Congressman George Bush (now U.S. Ambassador to the United Nations) once testified to "... the tremendous problems the members of my committee, Ways and Means, are faced with in attempting to obtain an accurate count of those persons eligible for Medicare when the undercount from 1960 is substantial for this age group." *Hearings,* May 8, 1969, *op. cit.,* p. 222.

local governments perform their newly acquired functions, significant new costs could be ascribed to errors in the statistical information that local authorities are required or find it expedient to use.

Last, systematic underenumeration and related sources of census error are likely to grow more important as major census users intensify their interest in relatively short-term changes in the social and demographic structure of small-area populations.[11] To cite one illustration, the Department of Labor has begun to seek ways of adding to existing statistical information bearing on the problems of pockets of chronic unemployment and underemployment. The Department has evinced a special interest in such issues as the incidence of involuntary part-time employment; the duration of periods of joblessness; minority training and education needs; job-seeking behavior; and the enduring occupation, education, and income problems of American Indians, Mexican–Americans, and Puerto Ricans.[12] Some of the needed data are being collected by the Census Bureau through the Current Population Survey; other portions have been gathered through the experimental Urban Employment Surveys. In both cases, however, the task of obtaining an accurate picture of the size and characteristics of the small population segments for which coverage is needed is complicated by the likelihood of encountering information-soliciting problems similar to those that confront the census.[13]

The Need for Better Information about Census Uses

Being able to answer the broad question of how much underenumeration is curable depends to a considerable extent on first being able to determine how much underenumeration is tolerable. To answer that question, however, it is essential to know in greater detail than present information allows how census data are actually used. In

[11] A list of recent proposals will be found in Otis Dudley Duncan, *Toward Social Reporting: Next Steps* (New York: Russell Sage Foundation), 1969, p. 1.

[12] See, for example, U.S. Department of Labor, Manpower Administration, "An Agenda for Manpower Research," *1968 Manpower Report* (Washington, D.C.: U.S. Government Printing Office), 1968.

[13] For example, one tenth of the data derived from the personal interview portion of the Urban Employment Surveys was imputed on the basis of reports given by interviewed persons. See Earle J. Gerson, "Methodological and Interviewing Problems in Household Surveys of Employment Problems in Urban Poverty Neighborhoods," in *Proceedings of the Social Statistics Section of the American Statistical Association,* 1969, p. 22.

attempting to understand the public-policy implications of underenumeration, and of analogous census inaccuracies, it rapidly becomes
apparent that existing knowledge about census uses, while extensive,
is scattered and incomplete. There are several published lists of
federal, state, and local programs that use census statistics in the
allocation of public funds.[14] The complex process of designing a
decennial census—a process that includes consultation with the Congress, with other government agencies, with various private organizations, and with the Census Bureau's many advisory bodies—is guided
by knowledge and expectations about the uses to which the collected
data will be put.[15] However, there is no current, comprehensive
source, or compilation of sources, of descriptive information about
even those uses of census data that are required by federal statute.[16]
Nor is a continuing systematic review of the end uses of census
material now the responsibility of any established federal agency.
The Census Bureau is making efforts to keep abreast of user needs,[17]

[14] The lists include Peter M. Allaman, "Population-based Grants from State
to Local Governments, F.Y. 1962" (Washington, D.C.: U.S. Bureau of the
Census), July 1964; Peter M. Allaman, "Population-based Grants from the
Federal Government to the State and Local Governments, F.Y. 1963" (Wash-
ington, D.C.: U.S. Bureau of the Census), July 1964; Department of Health,
Education, and Welfare, *Catalog of HEW Assistance* (Washington, D.C.: U.S.
Government Printing Office), 1969; Library of Congress, Legislative Reference
Service, *Catalog of Federal Aids to State and Local Governments,* Prepared for
the Subcommittee on Intergovernmental Relations of the Senate Committee on
Government Operations (Washington, D.C.: U.S. Government Printing Office),
April 15, 1964, and its *Supplement,* January 4, 1965, and *Second Supplement,*
January 10, 1966; Office of Economic Opportunity, *Catalog of Federal Domes-
tic Assistance* (Washington, D.C.: U.S. Government Printing Office), April 1970;
Commonwealth of Massachusetts, Executive Office for Administration and
Finance, *Catalog of Federal Aid Programs Administered through Agencies of
the Massachusetts State Government* (Boston: Commonwealth of Massachusetts),
1964; and State of New York, Department of Audit and Control, *State Aid to
Local Government* (Albany: State of New York), September 1969.

[15] See, for instance, *Hearings, op. cit.*

[16] There are several published catalogs of federal and state programs. Some
provide descriptions of applicant eligibility requirements, a brief outline of the
allocation formula used, and an indication of the amount of money distributed
each year. However, no one catalog gives all such information, along with the
state redistribution formula, the statistical data source used during intercensal
years, and the amount of money actually expended, as opposed to the amount
appropriated, each year. Even when detailed financial statements are offered, the
information is usually several years old.

[17] See the series, *Census Use Study,* especially *Data Tabulation Activities,*
Report No. 3 (Washington, D.C.: U.S. Bureau of the Census), 1970.

but its day-to-day monitoring activities rely heavily on requests for special tabulations. Similarly, the Office of Management and Budget, which is responsible for administrative and budgetary coordination of the federal statistical system, lacks the funds and staff needed to undertake a systematic assessment of the present and potential demand for products of the federal data collection enterprise.

There should be a cumulative, up-to-date register of all statutory uses that are made of census data for the purpose of allocating government funds and developing basic social services, and the Census Bureau should take the lead in establishing such a list. Moreover, the register should be gradually expanded in the direction of including all identifiable, official governmental uses of census statistics, beginning, for example, with those that are required by administrative order, regulation, or customary practice, supplemented, wherever feasible, by information on the kinds and frequency of uses made in the private sector of the economy and by individuals engaged in scientific research.

By virtue of the major federal role in creating and stimulating census data uses and in encouraging uniform standards for collecting and analyzing social data more generally, the principal producers of official social statistics have incurred an obligation to stay closely informed of the many purposes served by the series they produce. Furthermore, given the scope of federal data-collection efforts, as well as the many newly created or recently identified requirements for census data, it is unwise not to make a determined effort to remedy deficiencies in present knowledge about the end uses of census statistics.

The Census Bureau and the Office of Management and Budget maintain considerable discretionary control over the kinds and quality of data sought, the manner of collection, and the form of publication. A register of census uses would thus provide a helpful instrument for identifying instances in which contemplated changes in the census, or in a census-related statistical series, would directly affect the legally specified data requirements of known users and their constituencies. It should also contribute directly to improving the program and management decisions of government statistical offices. It will help in organizing their smaller surveys, in streamlining their procedures for record keeping and data publication, in developing plans for shifts of emphasis or selective expansion of staff, and in supporting requests for budgetary appropriations.

Finally, a register of uses would direct attention to emerging data requirements, thereby encouraging early appraisal of the effect of incomplete or inaccurate census statistics on proposed decision-making and research uses of government statistics. This last point is particularly important, since some data needs most likely to be affected by large census inaccuracies—differential underenumeration, classification errors, incomplete reporting—are still to be anticipated. The uses of census data in the design and evaluation of large-scale social experiments, for example, have yet to be adequately identified and examined.

Development of the register should be phased. To try to make a thorough compilation quickly might prove excessively difficult and costly. From the outset, however, information on each identified use should cover at least the following items:

- *Source* (constitutional requirement, statute, regulation, customary practice)
- *Branch* (legislature, department, agency, judicial administration)
- *Level of user* (including state and local users in instances where federal money is distributed to the states for reallocation on the basis of federal or other formulae)
- *Data used* (specific items)
- *Substantive purposes* for which the data are used

Initially, some of the information will be obtained by inspection of government statutes and published regulations and by pulling together the internal expertise of the principal producer agencies. Later, it will probably be necessary to encourage some collaboration among federal agencies, state and local governments,[18] and private professional organizations, which may be willing and should be encouraged to assist in developing the register.[19]

[18] Parallel efforts may already be under way in some states. In 1967, the Wisconsin State Government Interagency Census Data User Group was formed to determine state agency requirements for census data. The work of the group was financed, in part, by a planning grant from the Department of Housing and Urban Development. See State of Wisconsin, Department of Administration, Bureau of State Planning, Information Systems Section, *Preliminary Report on 1970 Census of Population in Wisconsin, Document No. BSP-IS-70-1* (Madison, Wisconsin), July, 1970.

[19] The Census Bureau has already issued at least one public invitation to demographers "to take a hard look at the uses to which they put the statistics of censuses and surveys and to make realistic appraisals of the accuracy requirements for the types of analyses for which the statistics are employed." See Barbara A. Powell and Leon Pritzker, "Effects of Variation in Field Personnel on Census Results," *Demography*, 2, 1965, p. 8.

It would be presumptuous to make a judgment at this time as to the most appropriate source of funding for the project. The Census Bureau can and should initiate the work, but it may be that responsibility for maintaining and expanding the register should eventually be assumed by the Office of Management and Budget. The Office, by virtue of its unique role in the federal system, is in by far the best position to make more people in more agencies and at more levels of government aware of the implications of census deficiencies and to assure that the register is adequately funded and maintained.

Analysis of the Effects of Census Underenumeration

Compilation of a register of census uses will provide information about the range of purposes that official social statistics serve, but it will not offer more than impressionistic insights into the practical effects of incomplete or inaccurate statistics on even those policy, decision-making, and research uses that can be readily identified. Accordingly, in addition to establishing and maintaining the recommended register, *the Census Bureau and other interested departments and agencies (including those that are not prime statistics producers) should also provide support for a series of case studies of the manner in which census data are used in the statutory allocation of federal, state, and local revenues and of the changes in those allocations that would result as a consequence of adjusting the data to account for various hypothesized rates of census undercounting.*

For example, black males are thought to be disproportionately undercounted. If the fact is that 20 percent of them are missed, and if the missed individuals are spread over the country in proportion to the distribution of counted persons in the same race–age–sex category, what are the consequences with regard to the magnitude and distribution of funds appropriated for job-training programs, either by the federal government or by the states? What are the consequences if only 10 percent are missed, or if the geographic distribution of undercounted black men is not proportionate to that of the counted black population in various age categories?

As the case studies would be selected from the recommended register of census uses, the immediate focus would be on governmental programs that distribute sizable sums of money in accordance with formulae that must, by law, be based at least in part on census statistics. However, the initial emphasis on large fund allocations should not be interpreted as a judgment that the amount of money disbursed in any one use of census data is necessarily the best measure of its importance. The impact of underenumeration on the allocation of lesser sums by cities, counties, school districts, or other communities may be very strong, and its consequences most serious. Nor should the initial stress on allocative uses be regarded as prejudging the importance of other governmental, business, or academic uses of census statistics.

The advantage of a series of studies confined, at the beginning, to the distributive uses of census statistics is that they can contribute to an estimate of the marginal benefit that would come from improvement of a given percent in census coverage. Where the reasonably estimated benefit was large, presumably the resources required to produce better statistics would be more readily forthcoming. If it were shown that particular areas of the country would derive tangible benefits from a reduction in or improved estimate of census undercounting, those areas would have a strong reason to cooperate more fully than they now do in assuring that the census is as complete as possible. If the uses and accuracy requirements of census data could be made clear in several important instances, both the Bureau of the Census and the Office of Management and Budget should be in a better position than they now are to determine the kinds of census data that are required at various levels of government and the form in which they would most usefully be provided.

It may be, for example, that existing federal, state, and local formulae for allocating public funds should be replaced by other measures. Present grant programs based on per capita income statistics might be made more effective if the income measure were coupled with a population factor adjusted for underenumeration. Work training and unemployment compensation programs might be made more responsive to the needs of their target populations if the impact of underenumeration on the allocative formulae used in the program could be made explicit.

It is important to note that local-area population counts are surrogate measures for most per capita allocations. One reason that allocations may not be well matched to need is that people who are counted, and who therefore serve as the basis for public fund distribution, may be the very ones who are leaving many affected areas, while those who remain behind, the principal beneficiaries of many government programs, are the most difficult to count. A consequence of the proposed analysis of the sensitivity of uses to underenumeration might thus be the proposal of alternative formulae that would be more sensitive to the actual counts of potential beneficiaries, or possibly a proposal that allocations now made on the basis of population be made according to some other criterion.

Over the long term, analysis of the effect of underenumeration on a set of major allocative census uses could also lead to analysis of the effect of other kinds of statistical deficiencies. What are the consequences, for instance, of classifying an individual improperly, counting an individual more than once, incorrectly estimating the existing number of individuals of a particular type (e.g., imputations and intercensal estimates, where there is no attempt to enumerate the population directly), or of erroneously predicting the number of individuals in certain categories at some future time (population projections)?

It is possible to envisage the proposed sensitivity analysis as leading to a useful series of less closely related policy studies focused on the manner in which states and localities develop programs that make them eligible for federal assistance and on the reasons that some grant-in-aid programs fail to achieve their intended objectives. Consideration of the allocation of grants by formula very quickly raises questions not only about the sensitivity of grant-in-aid formulae themselves but also about the manner in which they are selected and the rigor with which they are applied. Serious questions are being asked today about the amount of federal aid that actually reaches the target populations for which it is intended, but very little is known about *intra*state fund distributions. The redistributive consequences of public policy, and of factors associated with different standards and kinds of equity and efficiency, are only now becoming subjects of systematic research.[20]

---

[20] Reapportionment studies are a case in point. Early research on the observable, or predicted, consequences of *Baker* v. *Carr* (1962) and *Kirkpatrick* v. *Preisler* (1967) indicated that more equitable apportionment would probably have very little effect in such policy areas as taxation, welfare, education, health, and highway construction. See, for example, Thomas R. Dye, *Politics, Economics, and the Public* (Chicago, Illinois: Rand McNally & Company), 1966. Yet, recent work has begun to identify specifiable conditions under which such "political variables" can be seen to have measurable and significant consequences for the public policy process and its present or anticipated products. See, for example, Allan G. Pulsipher and James L. Weatherby, Jr., "Malapportionment, Party Competition, and the Functional Distribution of Governmental Expenditures," *American Political Science Review*, LXII(4), December 1968, pp. 1207–1219; and Brian R. Fry and Richard F. Winters, "The Politics of Redistribution," *American Political Science Review*, LXIV(2), June 1970, pp. 508–522. The last concludes that the proportion of families with less than $3,000 annual income is

The case studies will, of course, bring to light only a portion of the total effect of underenumeration on government programs. It may also be discovered that the programs most affected are at the state level. Total state grants to localities now exceed federal grants to the states, and state grants-in-aid also seem to be made more frequently on the basis of less complex formulae.[21] But if the first case studies are of large programs that are intended to have significant consequences, they are likely to indicate a need not only for continuing present research efforts but also for increasing expenditures on the census and related work.

In selecting formulae and programs to be studied, attention should be given to the known variety of statutory uses. There are, for example, program participation requirements and funding ceilings in which small-area population totals are the principal variable, but where the cutoff points are so widely spaced that, for some communities to be affected, coverage deficiencies would probably have to be substantial. There are allocation formulae in which population totals are broken down into categories differentiated according to one or more relevant attributes (often the age) of a target population. In such cases, substantial underenumeration of particular categories of a state's population could affect the distribution of federal money, but the most serious effects would probably be felt in instances in which a state's internal redistribution formula followed the federal pattern closely.

There are also eligibility standards and allocation formulae based on simple ratios of one or two subgroup characteristics within small-area populations,[22] as well as multivariate distribution formulae and

---

not related, as had been hypothesized, to more equitable distribution of state expenditures, regardless of region (pp. 520–521). The authors suggest that "redistribution to the lowest income classes is more a function of participation by these classes *than of their size* [emphasis added]."

[21] Thus, beginning June 25, 1971, 10½ percent of New York State's total personal income tax collections each state fiscal year will be shared by all cities in the state in existence as of April 1, 1968, on the basis of the percentage that the total population of the individual city represents of the total population of all cities in the state. State of New York, Office for Local Government *Newsletter*, IX:8, May 18, 1970, p. 1.

[22] Illustrations include surplus food distribution, in which the identification of eligible counties is made on the basis of income data from the most recent decennial census (*Hearings, op. cit.,* p. 6), and modest federal support of a range of public health services on the basis of small-area per capita income statistics. U.S. Public Health Service, Health Services and Mental Health Administration, *Grants*

complex eligibility criteria that, in some cases, because of the number of characteristics included, may well diminish the effects of any one particular source of data error. For example, support for a community action program is tendered to areas with a high incidence of poverty as measured by specified criteria, such as the concentration of low-income families, the persistence of chronic unemployment, the number of persons receiving welfare assistance, the number of migrant or transient poor, school dropout rates, and the prevalence of disease, disability, and infant mortality.[23]

Finally, there are allocation formulae in which, though population or some other descriptive measure is a principal component, the complexity of the formulae, or stipulations attached to them, appears to reduce the effect of any likely data error. Two examples are the Vocational Rehabilitation Act, as amended, and the Waste Treatment Works Construction Program under the Water Quality Act of 1965. In the former, the statutory allocation formula calls for multiplication of the population of each state by the square of its allotment percentage (a per capita income figure). The ratio of the product to the sum of all the corresponding products for all states then determines the proportionate share for each state.[24] In the latter, one half of the first $100 million of each yearly appropriation is allotted among the states in proportion to population, with the remainder being allocated on the basis of per capita income. However, allotted sums not obligated within a specified period are subject to reallotment to other states or to use for projects in which the need for sewage treatment facilities is partly attributable to the presence of a federal installation or federal construction activity.[25]

Each of these categories of funding criteria would be affected in different ways by different margins of error in different kinds of census data. Some would be vulnerable only to deficient population counts; others to errors in income or education statistics arising from systematic undercoverage of specific population subgroups. Each, moreover, could well suggest a different measure of error cost, because of great differences in the sums involved.

to *States for Public Health Services, Section 314 (d), Public Health Service Act,* Regulations, July 1, 1968, p. 8.

[23] *Catalog of Federal Aids to State and Local Governments, Supplement, op. cit.,* p. 27.

[24] *Catalog of Federal Aids to State and Local Governments, Second Supplement, op. cit.,* p. 176.

[25] *Ibid.,* p. 174.

Detailed understanding of the end uses of census statistics will not guarantee that better statistics will be used competently. Public programs are subject to many influences that have little to do with the quality of the statistics they use. Some grants are awarded to states with "good" proposed programs, rather than to others with the greater, statistically demonstrable, need. Other programs are not sufficiently funded to reach even their known target populations. Still others are politically vulnerable, or protected, or are required to use census statistics whose age is likely to introduce more distortions into a grant formula than any likely degree of undercounting. Also, as the Census Bureau discovered in its New Haven Census Use Study, many typical community groups and local governments do not yet fully understand how to use relevant census data beyond the statistics on total population, age, sex, and household relationships.[26] Nevertheless, the likelihood is that better use of statistics would be encouraged by the availability of better statistics.

[26] U.S. Bureau of the Census, *Census Use Study*, Report No. 3, *op. cit.*, p. 17. See also Todd M. Frazier, "The Questionable Role of Statistics in Comprehensive Health Planning," *American Journal of Public Health*, 60, September 1970, pp. 1701–1705.

2 Who Are the Uncounted People?

Net underenumeration in the Censuses of 1950, 1960, and 1970 is estimated on the basis of findings produced by three independent methods: postcensal re-enumeration in a sample of geographic areas, record-matching samples, and demographic analysis. In the case of the third, which is now the preferred method of evaluating census coverage, estimates are developed by comparing census totals with expected population figures derived from analysis of the results of previous censuses and from separate records of births, deaths, immigration, and emigration.

Demographic methods are inexpensive to use. Their limitations arise primarily from the lack of adequate migration data. The other methods, though usually more informative, are costly and have specific technical weaknesses. For example, experience has shown that the carefully controlled, intensive interviewing procedures of a special postcensal survey, while useful for identifying *completely unenumerated households,* are not much more likely than standard census procedures to find *persons missed within enumerated living quarters.* Similarly, although record matching is immensely useful for assessing the reliability and validity of information provided by enumerated households, there is reason to suspect that record linkage techniques may never provide acceptable estimates, at reasonable cost, of the error in census counts of persons.

Matching technologies, still relatively poorly developed, will be improved and made less expensive. However, there is the added difficulty that, for some persons, not being counted in a census may be symptomatic of not being listed in any other comparable record system. Whether it is ethically desirable to use matching techniques extensively is also open to question. Reinterviews and record matching were both used to evaluate coverage in the 1950 and 1960 Censuses. In 1970, in contrast, reinterviews were used only for measuring the quality of responses actually elicited by the 1970 Census questions, and record matching for coverage estimation purposes was limited to those few selected instances where opportunities existed for comparison with record systems, such as Medicare, that are believed to offer relatively thorough coverage of specific population categories.

Demographic Characteristics of the Underenumerated

Undercount estimates derived from demographic analyses are, of course, affected by errors in previous censuses, by imperfect vital statistics, and particularly by flawed immigration and emigration statistics. Nevertheless, demographic methods provide relatively inexpensive evidence of deficiencies in the national counts for many groups.[1]

---

[1] For detailed expositions of the estimation methods used, see Ansley J. Coale, "The Population of the United States in 1950 Classified by Age, Sex, and Color—A Revision of Census Figures," *Journal of the American Statistical Association,* 50, 1955, pp. 16–54; Morris H. Hansen, Leon Pritzker, and Joseph Steinberg, "The Evaluation and Research Program of the 1960 Censuses," *Proceedings of the Social Statistics Section of the American Statistical Association,* 1959, pp. 172–180; Conrad Taeuber and Morris Hansen, "A Preliminary Evaluation of the 1960 Censuses of Population and Housing," *Proceedings of the Social Statistics Section of the American Statistical Association,* 1963, pp. 56–73; U.S. Bureau of the Census, *Evaluation and Research Program of the U.S. Censuses of Population and Housing, 1960: Record Check Studies of Population Coverage,* Series ER60, No. 2 (Washington, D.C.: U.S. Government Printing Office), 1964; Melvin Zelnik, "Errors in the 1960 Census Enumeration of Native Whites," *Journal of the American Statistical Association,* 59, 1964, pp. 437–459; Jacob S. Siegel and Melvin Zelnik, "An Evaluation of Coverage in the 1960 Census of Population by Techniques of Demographic Analysis and by Composite Methods," *Proceedings of the Social Statistics Section of the American Statistical Association,* 1966, pp. 71–85; Melvin Zelnik, "An Examination of Alternative Estimates of Net Census Undercount by Age, Sex, and Color," Paper contributed to the Annual Meeting of the Population Association of America, New York, N.Y., April 1966; Jacob S. Siegel, "Completeness of Coverage of the Nonwhite Population in the 1960 Census and Current Estimates, and Some Implications," in David M. Heer (Ed.), *Social Statistics and the City* (Cambridge, Massachusetts: Harvard University Press for the Joint Center for Urban Studies of the Massachusetts Institute of Technology and Harvard University), 1968, pp. 13–54; and Jacob S. Siegel, "Coverage of Population in the 1970 Census: Preliminary Findings and Research Plans," Paper presented at the Annual Meeting of the American Statistical Association, Detroit, Michigan, December, 1970.

Table 1 presents such an estimate of the number of uncounted persons in the 1960 Census by sex, color, and age. The percentages are most reliable for persons under 25, since birth and death registration areas covered the entire United States only after 1933. For other ages, the soundness of the figures depends on the choice of demographic techniques used, the adequacy of assumptions made in applying those techniques, and the quality of the basic demographic data employed. Typically, Table 1 indicates that although, in absolute numbers, more whites than nonwhites[2] were missed by the 1960 Census, the estimated number of uncounted nonwhites, as a percentage of the total estimated nonwhite population, was disproportionately large (about 10 percent). Moreover, approximately 15 percent of all nonwhite males between the ages of 20 and 40 are estimated not to have been counted, with the highest proportion (20 percent) in the 25–29 age group. Similar patterns can be observed among females. While women in both color groups were generally more completely enumerated than men in corresponding age categories, nonwhite females were noticeably less well enumerated than white females, not only at ages over 45 (at which nonwhite females appear to have been even less well counted than nonwhite males) but also in the age groups in which nonwhite men were markedly undercounted.

Social Characteristics of the Underenumerated—Three Hypotheses

The reasons for the persistence of undercounting from one census to the next, and for the greater underenumeration of nonwhites, especially young nonwhite males, are not known. Three hypotheses, derived largely from census field experience and research, have strongly influenced recent thinking about the problem. One directs attention to incomplete reporting of the number of persons attached to enumerated living quarters; another centers on the possibility that un-

[2] In 1960, the color category "nonwhite" included Negroes, Indians, Japanese, Chinese, Filipinos, Aleuts, Eskimos, Hawaiians, part-Hawaiians, Asian Indians, Koreans, Malayans, and other racial or ethnic groups of non-European or non-Near Eastern origin. An explanation of the concept of race, as used by the Census Bureau in 1960, will be found in U.S. Bureau of the Census, *Characteristics of Population, 1960 Census of Population,* Part I, "U.S. Summary" (Washington, D.C.: U.S. Government Printing Office), November 1963, p. xli. Since Negroes comprise over 90 percent of all nonwhites in the United States, the 1960 count of nonwhites is often used to represent the Negro population. In 1970, however, separate tabulations will normally be made for whites, Negroes, and "other races."

TABLE 1   Estimated Amount and Percentage of Net Underenumeration of the Population by Age, Sex, and Color, in the 1960 Census[a]

Sex and Age	White, 1960 (April 1)		Nonwhite, 1960 (April 1)	
	Amount (thousands)	Percentage[b]	Amount (thousands)	Percentage[b]
Male, all ages	2,256	2.8	1,218	10.9
0–4	177	2.0	124	7.7
5–9	205	2.4	78	5.7
10–14	194	2.5	59	5.2
15–19	233	3.8	114	12.5
20–24	209	4.3	133	17.5
25–29	208	4.2	150	19.7
30–34	167	3.1	138	18.0
35–39	142	2.5	107	14.5
40–44	97	1.9	82	12.8
45–49	77	1.6	69	11.5
50–54	159	3.6	97	17.8
55–59	15	0.4	25	5.9
60–64	97	3.0	31	9.7
65 and over	276	3.8	11	1.8
Female, all ages	1,297	1.6	924	8.1
0–4	102	1.2	101	6.4
5–9	126	1.6	66	4.8
10–14	108	1.5	47	4.2
15–19	144	2.4	91	10.1
20–24	121	2.4	75	9.6
25–29	68	1.4	67	8.7
30–34	32	0.6	46	5.9
35–39	−11	−0.2	47	6.2
40–44	−11	−0.2	42	6.4
45–49	35	0.7	52	8.4
50–54	194	4.2	103	18.2
55–59	62	1.6	45	10.0
60–64	151	4.2	50	14.1
65 and over	176	2.1	92	12.2

[a]Reprinted with permission from Jacob S. Siegel, "Completeness of Coverage of the Nonwhite Population in the 1960 Census and Current Estimates, and Some Implications," in David M. Heer (Ed.), *Social Statistics and the City* (Cambridge, Massachusetts: Harvard University Press for the Joint Center for Urban Studies of the Massachusetts Institute of Technology and Harvard University), 1968, Table 2, pp. 42–43.

[b]These percentages were computed in the following manner: For a particular sex–color–age category, let C represent the Census-reported count and let E represent the "corrected" population count. Then, the percentage is $\left(\frac{E-C}{E}\right) 100$. The numbers in the "Amount" columns are the values of $E-C$. Footnote 2 on page 16 of Siegel gives the sources for the E values.

counted persons may not reside in any place enumerated by standard census procedures; and a third concerns the urban–rural distribution of uncounted persons.

The 1950 and 1960 Census Post-Enumeration Surveys (PES), and the results of demographic analyses of those two censuses, provide evidence that in 1950 and 1960 incomplete coverage of whites, both male and female, stemmed in large measure from failure to enumerate entire households. The most important inference to be drawn from the Post-Enumeration Surveys and related work, however, is that white and nonwhite undercount patterns seem to have differed markedly. While 70 percent of the *whites* known to have been missed in the 1960 Census were subsequently found in completely missed households, only 30 percent of the uncounted *nonwhites* appear to have been missed because their entire households were missed.[3] This evidence, plus the additional observation that persons loosely attached to households, such as lodgers and members of extended families, are more likely to be missed by the census than household heads, wives, and children,[4] has led to speculation that a large majority of missed nonwhites are "either present but unreported in enumerated living quarters or . . . not staying in any kind of place covered by the census."[5]

The second hypothesis—that some individuals are not counted because they are not staying in conventionally enumerated places— receives support not only from the 1960 PES but also from a small body of evidence developed during tests of 1970 Census field operations. In the spring of 1967, the Bureau of Labor Statistics and the Bureau of the Census jointly initiated a pilot research program aimed at improving the quality of statistical information about residents of urban poverty areas. Part of the effort was designed to develop data on the labor force characteristics of persons thought to be inadequately represented in sample surveys, mainly black men between the ages of 20 and 50, by means of a procedure called the "casual setting interview." Experimental interviews were conducted during the New Haven, Connecticut, pretest of the 1970 Census and later in

[3] Leon Pritzker and N. D. Rothwell, "Procedural Difficulties in Taking Past Censuses in Predominantly Negro, Puerto Rican, and Mexican Areas," in David M. Heer (Ed.), *Social Statistics and the City* (Cambridge, Massachusetts: Harvard University Press for the Joint Center for Urban Studies of the Massachusetts Institute of Technology and Harvard University), 1968, p. 66.

[4] *Ibid.*, p. 64.

[5] *Ibid.*, p. 66.

conjunction with a full-scale census "dress rehearsal"[6] in Trenton, New Jersey.[7]

"Casual setting interviews," in the census context, are conducted in such places as bars and poolrooms and on street corners. Lists of the names and addresses of interviewed persons are compiled for later matching with census records to determine the enumeration status of each person contacted. In New Haven, the procedure consisted of an initial encounter between interviewer and respondent in a casual setting, followed by an attempt to find and reinterview persons who, by checking census lists, could be definitely identified as uncounted in the census pretest. In Trenton, time and budget limitations precluded a second interview, but the lack of follow-up was partially offset by the larger scope of the Trenton project and by the fact that less than one in six of the men whose names could not be matched in New Haven were subsequently locatable for follow-up interviews at addresses they had given to casual setting interviewers.[8]

The findings of the two studies cannot be interpreted as descriptive of all uncounted men in the areas in which the research was conducted (or, in the case of New Haven, as representative of the universe of potentially relocatable persons). Many uncounted individuals may not have frequented the particular casual settings in which interviews took place or may have deliberately avoided contact with the interviewers. Nevertheless, the evidence gathered by the two studies does suggest that men who could be identified as uncounted tended, in comparison with enumerated men, to be more poorly educated, to have fewer family ties, and to exhibit a marked proclivity

[6] The distinction between a "pretest" and a "dress rehearsal" is that no previously untried procedures are used in the latter.

[7] The Trenton study was actually funded by the Trenton Model Cities Agency.

[8] In a third related project, the Bureau of Labor Statistics (BLS) attempted to obtain household interviews with individuals identified from lists of workers in low-paying jobs in New York City. Results of all three studies have been summarized by Deborah P. Klein in "Determining the Labor Force Status of Men Missed in the Census," U.S. Bureau of Labor Statistics, *Special Labor Force Report 117* (Washington, D.C.: U.S. Government Printing Office), March 1970. An earlier report on the New Haven and New York experience will be found, along with a description of the BLS pilot research program, in U.S. Bureau of Labor Statistics, *Pilot and Experimental Program on Urban Employment Surveys, Report No. 354* (Washington, D.C.: U.S. Government Printing Office), March 1969.

for frequent changes of residence. In New Haven, only 33 percent of the uncounted group were married, compared with 57 percent of those who had been enumerated. In Trenton, the respective percentages were 35 and 58. In New Haven, 46 percent of the uncounted individuals interviewed a second time had lived at their present addresses only a year or less, compared with 12 percent of the enumerated. In Trenton, where length of time at present address was ascertained during the casual setting interview, the observed tendency was in the same direction, though less noticeable. The respective percentages were 14 and 9.[9]

It is not clear whether the more stable living arrangements indicated by the Trenton data simply reflect bias in the selection of persons to be interviewed or point to some underlying aspect of culture or social structure.[10] But the New Haven experience alone would seem to encourage further exploration of the "not staying in any place" hypothesis. Even though such individuals may, from time to time, stay in enumerated living quarters, their lack of regular attachments to such places makes it conceivable that neither they nor anyone else regard them as "usual residents" or, for that matter, as having "a usual residence elsewhere." It may well be that, for practical purposes, such persons should be considered "to live" on street corners and in bars, poolrooms, and other "casual settings" in which censuses are not customarily taken.

A third hypothesis about the social characteristics and circumstances associated with underenumeration posits a relationship between census field office difficulties and undercounting in urban areas. Results of the 1950 and 1960 Post-Enumeration Surveys suggested that failure to enumerate entire households occurred most often in the inner zones of large cities, where there is an abundance of multiunit housing structures, and in remote, sparsely populated

[9] Interestingly, however, a principal finding of the New Haven and Trenton studies was that "the labor force status of the undercount group was very much like the labor force status of their neighbors who were counted." Klein, *op. cit.,* p. 28.

[10] For example, one fifth of the Trenton respondents were recent immigrants from Puerto Rico. Differences in industrial and residential location patterns could also be a factor. A wise recommendation emanating from the casual setting interview research is that similar studies be carried out "in cities and towns of different sizes and with different racial compositions." *Pilot and Experimental Program on Urban Employment Surveys, op. cit.,* p. 27.

rural areas. Moreover, the 1960 Census Time and Cost Study revealed that

when urban block cities [i.e., cities of 50,000 or more inhabitants for which data were to be published by city block], urban nonblock cities, and rural areas were compared, urban block cities appeared to be the most difficult in which to take the Census. They had the lowest proportion of enumerations completed on the first visit, . . . the highest closeout rate, . . . and took the longest time to complete. . . .[11]

These observations, along with more recent reports of similar difficulties encountered by other survey organizations,[12] led the Census Bureau to hypothesize a possible connection between 1960 field office difficulties and 1960 undercounts by age, sex, and race. That such difficulties would grow in 1970 also seemed reasonable to expect in the light of Current Population Survey data indicating increasing Negro population densities in major urban centers,[13] and given what is known or suspected about the demographic and social consequences of Negro migration out of the rural South.[14]

---

[11] U.S. Bureau of the Census, "A Proposed Coverage-Improvement Program for the 1970 Census," Response Research Branch Report No. 67–14 (Unpublished), May 5, 1967, p. 2. In addition, field canvass records for the 1960 Census show that, while 98 percent of the enumeration had been completed by April 30, "the remaining two percent was not completed until mid-July. Lags were concentrated in New York, Chicago, Los Angeles, and several other large cities." Pritzker and Rothwell, op. cit., p. 70.

[12] See, for example, George Gallup's remarks in the *New York Times* of November 1, 1968: ". . . the difficulties of doing a scientific poll in Harlem are extreme. . . . The normal living patterns are completely disarranged. . . . They just don't want to talk to a stranger." Quoted in Earle J. Gerson, "Methodological and Interviewing Problems in Household Surveys of Employment Problems in Urban Poverty Neighborhoods," *Proceedings of the Social Statistics Section of the American Statistical Association,* 1969, p. 23.

[13] See U.S. Bureau of Labor Statistics and U.S. Bureau of the Census, "The Social and Economic Status of Negroes in the United States, 1969," *BLS Report No. 375,* and *Current Population Reports,* Series P–23, No. 29 (Washington, D.C.: U.S. Government Printing Office), 1970.

[14] See, for example, Pritzker and Rothwell, op. cit., p. 68:

> . . . a low sex ratio has been historically an urban phenomenon both for native whites and for Negroes. Although the observed consistently low urban sex ratios for whites as well as for Negroes may result from differential migration of women to cities, our conjecture is that relatively high underenumeration of males in urban areas also contributes to it. At any rate, it is clear that the observed decline in combined urban and rural Negro sex ratios, as measured, can be entirely accounted for by the rapid urbanization of the Negro population. Standardization based on the 1900 Census proportions of rural and urban population produces nearly identical sex ratios in every decade from 1900 to 1960.

Accordingly, in 1970, the Census Bureau invested several million dollars in special efforts to assure an accurate count of people living in economically depressed areas of large cities, principally in the North and Midwest.[15] There was no opportunity to conduct an independent test of the presumed relationship between field office difficulties and differential census undercounting, but the hypothetical connection seemed reasonable.[16] In census field operations, the crucial linkages are the incomplete household enumeration and the "close-out," wherein follow-up interviewers are instructed to collect information from neighbors about persons residing in households to which enumerators have failed to gain access after several attempts. Close-out cases in 1960 were relatively more numerous in cities with populations of 50,000 or more. The 1960 PES also indicated that one third of the persons identified by the PES as missed by the census within enumerated living quarters were indeed attached to households that had originally been enumerated by close-out.[17] However, the inability of the PES to add a large proportion of uncounted black persons to the 1960 Census totals did caution against associating field office difficulties with suspected urban undercounts, and the presumed relationship has, therefore, remained an open issue.

Indeed, as preparations for the 1970 Census proceeded, the Bureau continued to consider the possibility that a large portion of the 1960 undercount occurred in parts of the South.[18] To date, evidence on this point is inconclusive, and may be supported only by assumptions about the accuracy of census data on interstate and interregional migration. If sufficiently refined, however, undercount estimates for states could provide an independent basis on which the hypothesis

---

[15] The special efforts included (a) establishment of a corps of "community educators" six months in advance of the census; (b) use of publicity media and local organizations to heighten awareness that a census was being taken; (c) more intensive training and supervision of enumerators; (d) more extensive use of hourly-rate enumerators; (e) a special check of the completeness of the mail-out/mail-back address register; and (f) a "missed persons" campaign to identify persons who thought they were not counted, or whom others regarded as not likely to have been counted.

[16] The hypothesis was explored further, albeit with inconclusive results, by a Subcommittee of the Advisory Committee. For details, see Appendix B, pp. 130–138, below.

[17] Pritzker and Rothwell, *op. cit.*, p. 64.

[18] U.S. Bureau of the Census, "The Coverage-Improvement Program for the 1970 Census," Response Research Branch Report No. 69–9 (R) (Unpublished), July 22, 1969, p. 3.

that guided the choice of places for intensive enumeration in 1970 could be re-examined.

Finally, it is conceivable that very little of what is known or suspected about undercounting in 1960 is relevant to what occurred in the 1970 Census or will occur in the future. Population mobility can reasonably be thought to have impeded census operations in the North and Midwest 10 years ago, but, in 1970, the principal problems may have stemmed from the hostility and resistance of groups that find themselves trapped in decaying urban ghettos. Or it may be that the rapid growth of a number of southern cities during the last decade had important, though unanticipated, effects on the pattern of undercounting there. One of the most important lessons to be learned from the many attempts to achieve complete or nearly complete census coverage is that the census is inextricably embedded in a network of social relationships that are undergoing change sufficiently significant in scale to strain even the most carefully designed efforts to understand and reduce counting deficiencies.

Other Hypotheses about Census Undercounting

Much speculation about the causes of census underenumeration centers on the high incidence of undercounting among young black men. This focus, as noted earlier, is the result of a fairly recent confluence between exigent social policy concerns and census coverage priorities.[19] Following the 1950 Census, when the first comprehensive studies of census undercounting were completed and published,[20] speculation about the causes of underenumeration ranged more widely and led to an initial array of experiments and procedural changes that crisscrossed a wide spectrum of possibilities.

For example, a study of the completeness of census counts of infants was undertaken in 1950. Unexpectedly, the test revealed that in 80 percent of the cases where infants had been missed, their par-

---

[19] For an illuminating overview of the historical linkages between coverage priorities and public policy issues, see Hyman Alterman, *Counting People: The Census in History* (New York: Harcourt, Brace & World), 1969, especially Chapters 7 and 8.

[20] Coale, *op. cit.*, and U.S. Bureau of the Census, "The Post Enumeration Survey: 1950," Bureau of the Census Technical Paper No. 4 (Washington, D.C.: U.S. Government Printing Office), 1960. A number of earlier studies using demographic analysis had shown problems in the coverage of infants in the population census, not only in the United States but also in other parts of the world.

ents, often young adults living in the homes of relatives, had also been missed.[21]

Similarly, it has long been suspected that age-reporting errors account for a large proportion of what otherwise appear to be undercounts of persons over 50 years of age. The contention is that undercount estimates contain a net overstatement of the number of persons aged 65 and older, with a corresponding net understatement in the immediately preceding age categories. Modest research efforts have thus far produced no significant conclusions one way or the other, but the age-reporting hypothesis has never been completely discarded.[22]

Another line of inquiry that has been intensively pursued might be termed the "frictional undercount" hypothesis—that is, the contribution to errors in a census made by persons who are hired to collect and process census data under unusually heavy workload conditions. The experience of all survey research organizations attests to the advantages of having a corps of highly trained individuals to carry out the detailed operations that large household surveys characteristically involve. Moreover, a study of learning curves for Current Population Survey interviewers (who are permanent, part-time Census Bureau employees) "has shown that two and one-half years are required for an interviewer to achieve peak performance . . . as measured by noninterview rates and the frequency of edit [misclassification] problems. . . ."[23]

Such extensive on-the-job training is not possible for the thousands of enumerators who are hired to take the census once every 10 years. Numerous opportunities for error are also created by the rapid, short-term organizational expansion that each census requires. Consequently, the Census Bureau early concluded that underenumeration might well be due in part to deficiencies in its own field operations.

Two decades of procedural innovation, testing, and evaluation have, however, yielded fewer encouraging results than originally anticipated. Two post-enumeration surveys and several enumerator and coding variance studies have identified and measured census staff

---

[21] U.S. Bureau of the Census, *Infant Enumeration Study:* 1950, Procedural Studies of the 1950 Censuses, No. 1 (Washington, D.C.: U.S. Government Printing Office), 1953.

[22] Hansen and Taeuber have seriously questioned it, however. See Hansen and Taeuber, *op. cit.,* pp. 59–60.

[23] Gerson, *op. cit.*

contributions to reporting and tabulation errors, but the principal light they shed on the causes of undercoverage was the finding that enumerators missed more than half the estimated number of uncounted persons identified by the 1960 PES because they failed to canvass entire households. Such a finding was significant. It is one factor that accounts for the introduction of the census-by-mail in 1970, but it also has suggested to the Census Bureau that there are limits to the explanatory potential of what once appeared to be a most promising line of investigation.

There are aspects of frictional undercounting that still merit exploration. The 1970 Census evaluation program includes, for example, studies of the adequacy of the mail address register, of errors occasioned by misapplication of the census housing definition, and of reporting and tabulation inaccuracies. There has also been measurement of the errors associated with certain standard features of the census, such as the length of census questionnaires, and continuing discussion of the possible effects of the mandatory response requirement and of respondents' doubts about official assurances that census data on individuals will be held in strictest confidence.

The Census Bureau regards the two-stage enumeration procedure used in the 1960 Census as, in effect, a nationwide experiment with a shorter questionnaire that produced no substantial change in net undercoverage.[24] However, whether a different kind of short questionnaire would have produced different results remains a topic for further inquiry.

The mandatory response and confidentiality provisions have been examined only tentatively. It has been felt that the former is likely to encourage enumeration among the groups that are least well counted and that the second cannot be adequately studied until more is known about the social characteristics and distinguishing ways of life of uncounted persons. The government has rarely prosecuted anyone for failing to respond to census queries, and long experience with household surveys has convinced the Bureau that most people do not have to be persuaded to cooperate, *once they have been personally contacted by an enumerator.* The difficulty is that missed persons are, by definition, not contacted by anyone, anywhere, so

---

[24] In the 1960 Census, households were enumerated in two stages. In the initial round, respondents were asked to answer only the eleven basic demographic and housing questions. Longer sample questionnaires were not delivered until enumerators canvassed each household to retrieve the information on the short forms.

that it is impossible to know with certainty what may cause them to remain uncounted. Disclosure surely has different implications for illegal occupants of public housing than for middle-class citizens concerned about alleged government "snooping." So also, misreporting on income and other census items may be motivated by a variety of considerations corresponding to specific circumstances in which respondents find themselves or to their different perceptions of the uses of census data. But it remains a matter of conjecture whether what is known or might be learned about such circumstances and perceptions will prove in any way useful for understanding why the very existence of certain persons is overlooked or concealed.

The Importance of Multiple Lines of Inquiry

In retrospect, the limited explanatory capacity of so many common-sense hypotheses about the causes of underenumeration can be seen to have slowly turned attention away from alleged defects in census field operations toward closer examination of the social characteristics and hypothesized life ways of undercounted groups. The B L S– Census studies of uncounted men in New Haven and Trenton are symptomatic of the changed perspective. So, in fact, is the establishment of the Advisory Committee on Problems of Census Enumeration. Both reflect a tentative reformulation of the undercount problem in terms of adaptive human behavior associated with being poor, a victim of racial or social discrimination, and an inhabitant of blighted places seldom visited by the society's more affluent and more secure members.

It would, however, be unfortunate if the new cast of thinking were to lead to a narrowing of the range of hypotheses advanced or of the categories of undercounted persons to be considered. There is still insufficient evidence to warrant concluding that the majority of uncounted persons is to be found at one extreme of the economic spectrum, or to assert that being black makes a person less likely to be counted than, say, being poor or functionally illiterate, or even moderately wealthy and very mobile.

The attention recently focused on black undercounts is long overdue and should be maintained, but race should not be viewed as an explanatory variable of such overwhelming importance as to discourage investigation of other characteristics that more directly account for the exclusion of people from the census. While undercount estimates by age, sex, and race serve clear purposes in the collection and publication of official social statistics, they are not adequate guides for the design of research intended to improve census coverage. There is a danger, in other words, that the practice of presenting census undercount estimates by age, sex, and race will turn out to be an unfortunate example of the way in which data-classification frameworks affect thinking about social problems.

Several different factors are surely responsible for underenumeration. Hence, although the evidence of black undercoverage is dramatic, there is a need for research along other lines of investigation tied to different causal hypotheses. For example, an unexplained result of demographic analysis of census counts is that coverage of nonwhite females appears to decline as the cohorts age, while the pattern for nonwhite males is, also inexplicably, the reverse. The data hint, moreover, that not being counted, for both whites and Negroes, has something to do with being young and, therefore, perhaps relatively unencumbered by conventional social linkages that make the vast majority of the population readily locatable. Inquiry into the distinguishing characteristics and life styles associated with undercoverage of middle-aged black women and young adults would be worthwhile in itself and might also illuminate the enumeration problems of other categories of undercounted persons.

The need for multiple research approaches and complementary lines of inquiry should be strongly stressed. In later chapters of this report, several additional research approaches are recommended. However, both the Census Bureau and other sponsors and performers of census-related research should also rethink and rework the findings of previous studies of undercounting in the light of recent hypotheses. Census research and field reports suggest that data from the 1960 PES, for example, could be retabulated to provide greater information on the relationship between the social characteristics of "subsequently found" households and the social and behavioral characteristics of enumerators and other census field personnel who failed to count such households in the census but located them in the PES.

In addition, it is important to be aware of how the objectives and intellectual style of the research staffs of the Census Bureau and other agencies with an interest in enumeration problems appear to have affected past research on the census. Much of the evaluative research on the census during the last two decades has concentrated on developing statistical procedures and household interviewing methods that would improve the quality of the census generally. Hence, strong emphasis has been placed both on measuring the extent of systematic error and dispersion in the responses made to standard census queries by various groups in the population and on devising new enumeration techniques, such as the census-by-mail.

That work has been highly successful. Moreover, the basic mode of analysis is a powerful tool for many purposes, as the greatly improved quality of census statistics indicates. It seems reasonable to expect, however, that research on the census and on similar social data-gathering activities could be further improved by expanding the amount of attention given to the behavioral and social aspects of the enumeration process. The Census Bureau has already made a start in that direction, as indicated by its role in the casual setting interview studies and by its demonstrated interest in ethnographic research as a means of developing new hypotheses about the causes of census errors.[25] Nevertheless, development of behavioral and social science research perspectives could be more fully encouraged and should be made a more central feature of the overall census research effort.

[25] See pp. 94–97, below.

3   A Strategic Approach to Research on Census Coverage Problems

During the last two decades, the Bureau of the Census has worked vigorously to improve the overall quality of population census data. The Census Research and Evaluation Programs have had two principal objectives: obtaining an accurate count of the total population every 10 years; and improving the reliability and validity of information collected from or about persons identified in censuses and current surveys.

This strategic approach to census improvement has had several important consequences. For example, the Bureau has developed outstanding research competence in such fields as statistics, demography, and social survey methods. Its work in those fields has produced a number of highly valued methodological innovations. By the same token, however, the direct linkage between the Bureau's research effort and the operational objective of improving the *overall quality* of census data appears to have made it difficult for the Bureau to do, or to sponsor, research that aims primarily to explain why this or that kind of census error occurs. Moreover, partly because of the kinds of methodological competence given emphasis in the Bureau's evaluation programs, and partly because of limited understanding of the possible effects of census counting deficiencies (see Chapter 1), it has seldom been easy for the Bureau to draw directly on the full range of potential sponsors and performers of research related to census-taking problems.

This chapter is concerned with ways of augmenting those aspects of research on the census that relate to the social conditions and processes associated with underenumeration and other problematic aspects of social data collection. As indicated earlier (p. 5), a central recommendation emerging from the Committee's work is that the present conception of enumeration-related research should be broadened by adopting and purposefully pursuing research strategies that more strongly emphasize the relationship between census-taking problems, such as underenumeration, and the social contexts in which censuses and social surveys are conducted. However, before examining each of the several lines of inquiry proposed, it seems worthwhile to consider the several ways in which potential performers of such work can identify their common areas of research concern. If underenumeration and poverty are linked, for example, those responsible for counting the poor and those interested in understanding or alleviating the problems of the poor should have large areas of mutual research interest. Furthermore, as noted in earlier chapters, it appears that the effects of census errors may not only be potentially widespread and cumulative, but they may also pose procedural and analytical problems for all social survey activities and raise fundamental research questions of interest to many social scientists in different disciplines.

The following discussion is divided into two parts. In the first, studies undertaken in connection with the 1960 and 1970 Censuses of Population are examined with a view to lessons that can be learned from them in planning future research. In the second, new forms of research stimulation are suggested that, if adopted, should make it easier both to expand present conceptions of census-related research and to implement more readily the research recommendations advanced in later chapters.

Evaluation of the 1960 Census and Preparations for 1970

Research projects undertaken by the Census Bureau at the beginning of each decade naturally tend to focus on evaluation of the most recent census. Also, designed as they are primarily to measure the accuracy of the data that have been collected and to identify sources of data error,[1] they tend to use methods developed through repeated testing. The 1960 Census Evaluation and Research Program, for example, included the following kinds of projects: two response vari-

---

[1] U.S. Bureau of the Census, *Evaluation and Research Program of the U.S. Censuses of Population and Housing, 1960: Background Procedures and Forms,* Series ER 60, No. 1 (Washington, D.C.: U.S. Government Printing Office), 1963, p. 1.

ance studies (one focused on enumerators, the other on respondents); a coding variance study; a record check to measure undercoverage in the general population; record checks to measure undercoverage of special groups—mainly Social Security beneficiaries and college students; a re-enumerative study of coverage error (the 1960 Post-Enumeration Survey); a series of content error studies, involving both re-enumeration and record matching; and demographic analysis of the 1960 Census national totals.

Similarly, the 1970 Evaluation and Research Program, in addition to demographic analysis of the 1970 Census results, contains a Census–Medicare record-matching study to measure the accuracy of the census count of persons 65 and older; an evaluation of content accuracy through reinterview, along the same lines as in 1960, though focused on fewer items (see p. 92); a series of record checks— Current Population Survey, Internal Revenue, Immigration and Naturalization Service—also intended for content evaluation; and studies of the completeness of the address registers (on which the census-by-mail depends), of units reported vacant or deleted as non-existent by postmen and enumerators, and of definitional errors in the housing unit count. This list does not include all the items proposed for the 1970 Research and Evaluation Program, but it does cover the principal components and the largest claims on the research and evaluation budget.

Research projects focused on a forthcoming census, on the other hand, tend to occupy the Bureau during the latter half of each decade and to be of a different kind. Most are separate studies that proceed in stages, each more complex than its predecessor, until sufficient evidence has been gathered to justify a choice of format and organizational arrangements for the impending count. Once that point is reached, additional trials are undertaken in which special supplementary procedures are tested for possible later use in areas where enumeration problems are anticipated. These "intensive procedure" studies are usually proposed on the basis of experience gained during tests of standard enumeration procedures, but they may also be exploratory studies suggested by research of others on the characteristics of population subgroups identified by demographic analysis as least well counted in previous censuses.

To illustrate, after a series of pilot studies in the 1950's the mail-out/mail-back technique used in the 1970 Census was first field-tested on a substantial scale in Ft. Smith, Arkansas, in August 1961. It was found that respondents could fill out with reasonable accuracy and speed the kind of questionnaire that computer processing demands.[2] Next, in Louisville, Kentucky, in 1964, there was a more extensive test of the mail system, which sought primarily to evaluate the effectiveness of an address register (in this case, the 1960 Census address list updated by comparison with utility meter installations) for identifying all potentially contactable households. The Louisville project indicated that the mail procedure would reduce by half the number of "close-out" cases in a regular census. That is, it would reduce by half the number of households from which census information could not be obtained directly from any occupant.

The Louisville test was repeated in Cleveland, Ohio, in April 1965, using a commercial mailing list corrected and updated by mailmen and adding a query to the questionnaire on the number of households at each address. If the recorded answer indicated a larger number of households than the total identified by the mailing list, an enumerator was sent to check the discrepancy. As a consequence of these accumulated studies, the Census Bureau made a commitment to use the mail procedure for counting approximately 60 percent of the population in 1970.[3]

Once the decision to use the mail-out/mail-back procedure had been made, the remaining task became one of developing a set of supplementary intensive enumeration procedures to be tested and later used in "hard-to-enumerate" urban areas. The Louisville and Cleveland tests produced evidence that, although the mail system improved overall population coverage, both white and Negro, it did not substantially reduce deficiencies in the counts of black men. Moreover, while Post Office checks of listed housing units were

[2] The information in this section is taken primarily from two sources: Richard C. Burt, "Final Plans for the 1970 Census—How the Data Will Be Collected," a paper prepared for presentation at the American Statistical Association Annual Meeting, August 21, 1969; and Leon Pritzker and N. D. Rothwell, "Procedural Difficulties in Taking Past Censuses in Predominantly Negro, Puerto Rican, and Mexican Areas," in David M. Heer (Ed.), *Social Statistics and the City* (Cambridge, Massachusetts: Harvard University Press for the Joint Center for Urban Studies of the Massachusetts Institute of Technology and Harvard University), 1968, pp. 55–79.

[3] The mail procedure was tested at least three more times in New Haven, in Trenton, and in Dane County, Wisconsin. In Dane County, 90 percent of the mailed questionnaires were returned within 10 days. U.S. Bureau of the Census, "The Outlook for the '70 Census," Internal Memorandum, n.d., p. 2.

found to eliminate almost completely the number of missed housing structures, missed units *within* multiunit structures continued to be a chronic coverage problem.[4]

Accordingly, the Bureau initiated a series of intensive procedure studies, beginning with a test of follow-up evaluation methods in Memphis, Tennessee, in March 1967. The findings suggested that follow-up enumerators should be given smaller assignments, crew leaders smaller crews, and that ghetto residents hired as enumerators would benefit from more intensive training than had originally been planned.

The New Haven pretest and a special study of supplementary counting procedures in Philadelphia, Pennsylvania, followed. In New Haven, "casual setting interviews" were attempted for the first time, coupled with efforts to identify uncounted persons from Post Office change-of-address cards and school enrollment and labor recruitment lists. In Philadelphia, the special techniques tested were, for the most part, variations of the standard door-to-door enumeration and follow-up procedures that the Census Bureau has used in the past. In both cases, however, the research objective was to identify counting methods that singly, or in concert, would be sufficiently effective to warrant their use in the forthcoming Trenton "dress rehearsal," and later in the 19 cities in which "intensive enumeration areas" had been selected for the 1970 Census. The procedures tested in Philadelphia included a revised enumerator-selection-aid test, hiring high school students as enumerators, more intensive enumerator training and supervision, hourly (rather than piece-rate) payment of enumerators, a precanvass check of the test area address list, team enumeration, a word-of-mouth public information campaign, and an intensive, follow-up, "within-household" check for uncounted persons. The original plan also called for work with a community action agency, but that proposal was never implemented.

---

[4] In urban areas in 1960, "some 31 percent of occupied units . . . were in multiunit structures, but some 60 percent of *missed* occupied units were in enumerated, but miscounted, multiunit structures." Joseph Waksberg, "Housing Unit Coverage Errors by Type of Geographic Areas—1960 Census," Memorandum to Members of the Task Force on Coverage Evaluation, January 23, 1967, p. 2. Similarly, the address register used at the beginning of the Trenton dress rehearsal inadequately identified 21.2 percent of all units in multiunit addresses. U.S. Bureau of the Census, "1970 Census 'Dress Rehearsal' Program," Results Memorandum No. 41, April 2, 1969, p. 2.

The results of the New Haven and Philadelphia studies are instructive. Informal Post Office checks on known movers had been made previously in Louisville and Cleveland, with encouraging results, but in New Haven a more sytematic change-of-address study identified very few uncounted persons. The check of school enrollment and job applicant lists also yielded only a minute number of unenumerated individuals, and those at an estimated cost of $20 per added name.[5] In Philadelphia, the results were similarly discouraging.

> The combined effect of the efforts to make test-taking less threatening, training longer, supervision closer, and hourly payment was to reduce attrition of the staff to nearly zero. That meant, however, that the inefficient as well as efficient workers remained and the productivity was low. . . .
> The precanvass resulted in small but measurable coverage improvement and had desirable incidental effects of introducing trainees to their assigned areas . . . and of cleaning address registers in an area of extensive demolition for which the post office operation failed to account. . . .
> The within-household check for missed persons, however, was a failure. . . . The consensus of enumerator and observer opinion was that the problem was not misunderstanding who should be reported in the household but lack of belief in confidentiality of census reports.[6]

Decisions about the intensive enumeration procedures to be used in 1970 nonetheless had to be made. The task appears to have been further complicated by the fact that the three special procedure studies (Memphis, New Haven, and Philadelphia) had been essentially independent. Hence, they had differed markedly in scope, comparability, and in the hypotheses they examined. Loose threads had been left hanging on more than one occasion. Explanations for the apparent failure of one or more techniques frequently had to be inferred rather than derived from comparable research efforts under clearly specified experimental conditions. Mover checks, for instance, produced different results in Cleveland, Louisville, and New Haven, but, since the studies were not comparable in scope, there was no way of determining why the differences occurred. The "fear of disclosure" identified in Philadelphia was an unanticipated finding that could not

---

[5] The cost included a follow-up interview to establish the individual's actual existence and address. U.S. Bureau of the Census, "The Coverage Improvement Program for the 1970 Census," Internal Response Research Branch Report No. 69–9 (R) (Unpublished), July 22, 1969, p. 9.

[6] *Ibid.*, p. 10.

be compared with a like or different experience elsewhere. The unsuccessful school enrollment and job applicant checks in New Haven only permitted the Bureau to speculate that the matching efforts failed because the few unenumerated persons whose names were found on independent lists were people whose presence was not likely to be acknowledged at any address given for them on a matched list.[7]

There are, of course, valid reasons why some of the testing and exploratory work appears to have produced such tentative or ambiguous results. As noted earlier, most of the research was, first of all, part of an effort to develop and evaluate a new method of census taking that would be generally usable. The census-by-mail, based on a controlled advance listing of contactable addresses, was a significant innovation. It was intended to reduce the number of completely missed households and to improve the quality of responses to census queries. It drew upon earlier research that had identified the door-to-door enumerator as a major contributor to response and coverage error. But, given the novelty of the procedure, a prime objective of the research effort was to devise procedures for assuring that the address-register/mailed-questionnaire procedure would not *lower* the level of coverage and accuracy achieved by conventional methods in 1960.

Second, it is understandable that in its initial efforts to deal with the undercount problem, the Bureau has concentrated on variables customarily considered to be within its control and on methodologies that are familiar and sufficiently developed to encourage confidence in the findings they produce. Third, it appears that the Bureau, constrained by limited research budgets, must often settle for multipurpose, nonreplicative, exploratory studies. Hence, the Bureau tends to do what it knows how to do and to do that best. Fourth, the preparatory work for the 1970 Census, like much of the research on the population census during the last 20 years, was a process of discovering how difficult it is to maintain high census-taking standards. The Bureau consequently sought, step by step, to develop new methods of dealing with each new problem as it arose or was identified, while remaining constantly mindful of the need to translate research findings directly into operational enumeration procedures.

[7] *Ibid.*, p. 8.

Some Possible Lessons of the 1970 Experience

Important lessons for the future can be learned from the preparations for the 1970 Census, quite apart from whatever knowledge was gained about the effectiveness of specific field procedures. One of the most important is surely that a problem like under-enumeration requires a broad research perspective and a broadly based research effort. The Census Bureau is exceptional among government organizations in the continuity of its research interest and in the cumulative nature of its research undertakings. Yet, as the Bureau well knows, most of the advances in data collection methods that it has pioneered during the last two decades are the fruits of intensive work by statisticians on the theory and applications of survey methods, with particular emphasis on studies of measurement accuracy.[8] The Bureau has, in effect, been trying to develop scientifically objective approaches to evaluating the quality of census and social survey data—approaches that would enjoy the same high regard as comparable measurement techniques in the natural sciences.[9]

This is an ambitious objective. The Bureau, moreover, can be justifiably proud of the large innovative role it has played in developing and refining social survey procedures and their attendant modes of data analysis. Yet the Bureau's attention has been sharply focused on one research instrument—the census questionnaire—and on one research framework—the various methods of delivering, retrieving, and interpreting completed census forms. Research and evaluation efforts in this context have produced important findings, most notably the sizable enumerator contribution to response variance. But, as the Bureau becomes increasingly concerned with the enumeration problems of small population subgroups, styles of problem definition and research design that have served it well in the past may become less productive of manageable solutions to census-taking deficiencies.

Another lesson lies in the limitations on what can be tried in the process of preparing and taking a decennial census. In the past, it has

[8] See, for example, Leon Pritzker and Joseph Waksberg, "Changes in Census Methods," *Journal of the American Statistical Association,* 64, December 1969, pp. 1141–1149.
[9] See Joseph F. Daly, "Some Basic Principles of Statistical Surveys," *Journal of the American Statistical Association,* 64, December 1969, pp. 1129 and 1133.

usually proved feasible for the Census Bureau to test major innovations under actual census conditions before adopting them in subsequent censuses. There is the ever-present danger, however, that an experimental procedure may prolong an enumeration unduly, or even adversely affect the counts in certain areas. The Bureau also can lack sufficient control of its field operations where complete control might otherwise be expected. For example, even if the Bureau were to find that enumerators of a certain age had the highest performance rate on the selection-aid tests, or in a census pretest, it could not use a narrow age criterion as a basis for hiring.[10] It could even be criticized for undertaking certain kinds of experiments. Because of its candor in acknowledging the existence of an undercount problem, the Bureau has recently been under pressure "to reduce the burden" on census and survey respondents, the assumption being that by making fewer inquiries more accurate and more complete information will be elicited.

Finally, although the Bureau has learned a number of interesting facts about underenumeration in the course of trying to improve the census generally, the approach that has been followed in the past tends to precipitate questions such as: What proportion of records can be linked? What kinds can be linked? What kinds cannot be linked? Answers to such questions reveal much about the magnitude of the problem, but they provide few insights into its dynamics—into the process that produces the effect.

During the 1970's, for example, the Bureau apparently intends to test alternative forms of the census questionnaire. The tests have been proposed because several small experiments in the 1960's suggested that there may be some advantages to using a questionnaire different from the one employed in the 1970 Census. The Bureau plans, however, to measure the joint effects of alternate formats and question wordings on (a) response rates (as a function of time interval between mail-out and receipt); (b) completeness and internal consistency of response (leading to estimates of number requiring follow-up); and (c) accuracy of responses.[11] In other words, the studies, as they have

---

[10] Barbara Bailer and Gail Inderfurth, "Questionnaires for the Enumerators Included in the Enumerator Variance Study of 1970," U.S. Bureau of the Census Internal Memorandum No. E-18, No. 9, September 24, 1969, p. 2. See also Robert H. Hanson and Eli Marks, "The Influence of the Interviewer on the Accuracy of Survey Results," *Journal of the American Statistical Association*, 53, September 1958, pp. 635–655.

[11] U.S. Bureau of the Census, "Effect of Questionnaire Wording and Design

been described by the Bureau, will measure questionnaire effectiveness in terms of operating expenditures required to achieve given levels of response quality, rather than being used also to find out *why it is* that one format elicits a greater number of more rapid or more accurate responses than another.

Inferences can be drawn from the measures the Bureau plans to use in its questionnaire experiments. The level of literacy required to complete one form may appear to be considerably lower than that required by another. The wording of questions in some instances may seem to be more in line with the conceptions of "residence," "marital status," or "head of household" held by large numbers of people interviewed. But, while measurement of response rates, and of the errors occasioned by alternative enumeration instruments, will continue to provide estimates of the relative cost and benefit of whatever procedures are tried, it will never explain the causes of error, nor will it indicate whether the procedures studied are, in fact, those that are well suited to achieving their intended purposes.

Developing Additional Research Capacity

In planning future research on underenumeration and other social data-gathering problems, *more emphasis should be placed on developing new conceptual frameworks for the exploration of phenomena not usually perceived as relevant to the organized process of collecting census and survey information.* One approach would be to adopt a research perspective like that proposed in Chapter 4, which directs attention to social–psychological problems arising at points where census purposes and procedures intersect with the customary events and circumstances of everday life. *Moreover, operationally, the Census Bureau and other potential research sponsors should actively seek to broaden the base of social science knowledge and training to which the Bureau has access.*

There are essentially three directions that the Bureau could take in pursuit of an expanded social science research capacity. It could develop a larger and more heterogeneous external research constituency; broaden the composition of its professional staff; and provide opportunities for continuing consultation with groups of scientists

---

on Accuracy and Public Cooperation," *Proposed Evaluation and Research Program for the 1970 Census of Population and Housing,* Census Bureau memorandum (Unpublished), January 1969, p. 18.

drawn from fields in which the Bureau would like to stimulate an interest in data collection and use problems.

External Research Communities Expansion of the number and variety of relationships that the Bureau maintains with external research communities and with different kinds of external research institutions would serve several purposes. First, there are certain kinds of work on the census that can be appropriately done by outside researchers or research organizations or that, if undertaken externally, might bring added strength, either because of limitations on Bureau staff capacity and expertise or because the nature of the project calls for maximum flexibility and independence from actual census-taking operations.

Second, as the Bureau becomes increasingly involved in exploratory substantive research and experimentation, it will encounter a corresponding need to invest in efforts to enrich the base of fundamental behavioral and social science knowledge bearing on the enumeration process. Staff with operating and research responsibilities linked to established data-collection programs cannot be expected to concern themselves deeply with attempts to define their problems differently or to develop radically different modes of achieving their program objectives. Consequently, the Bureau will need to support external research that both encourages and facilitates extension of the range of operational variables considered to be within its control. In some cases, this will require support of work that is clearly related to the enumeration process as presently conceived, such as research to develop new ways of measuring the reliability and validity of respondent perceptions and attitudes. In others, it will involve work that explores areas whose immediate relevance to census taking is less evident, or where the directions in which to proceed are not presently well illuminated by scientific understanding. Since a large fraction of the knowledge and skills required for such research will be found among social and behavioral scientists located in academic settings, the Bureau will need to strengthen and enlarge the variety of incentives that it can offer to outside researchers.

Last, external research should be supported with a view to stimulating awareness of and interest in the potential consequences of census-data deficiencies, both within the academic community and at the several levels and branches of government. By being mindful of the training opportunities associated with the support of outside research, and by attempting to engage state and local governments in the task of organizing and funding census-related studies, the Bureau can substantially increase the manpower and budgetary resources available for work that will lead to improvements in census-data quality. State and local participation in developing a register of data uses, as well as in studies of data-error effects, would be particularly appropriate and useful. So would intergovernmental and interagency involvement in research that explores the degree of congruence between the information provided by existing data-gathering instruments and what it is that census users actually want to know about the characteristics of the population. Studies of the registration of vital events, of mail-delivery procedures, and of record-matching techniques suggest several easily exploitable opportunities to encourage cooperative research involvement. There are also evident dispositions and precedents for multiagency participation in support of more fundamental research, such as interviewing and ethnographic studies.[12]

Of the several ways in which the Bureau can proceed toward strengthening and expanding its ties with external research communities, one would be to announce its strong receptivity to unsolicited proposals forthcoming from research areas not conventionally associated with enumeration and survey research. Another would be to provide support by grant, contract, or joint statistical agreement[13] to one or more departments, schools, or university-based research centers that would agree to restructure or expand their present research concerns and resources so as to provide social and behavioral science

[12] The joint Bureau of the Census–Bureau of Labor Statistics sponsorship of "casual setting interview" studies has been mentioned. The jointly sponsored (Census Bureau–National Center for Health Statistics) study of health survey interviewers is yet another example. See below, pp. 72 and 89. In addition, the Department of Labor and the Department of Housing and Urban Development have seriously considered, but have not yet implemented, programs of support for ethnographic studies in poverty areas. The Advisory Committee on the Census (1970), established by New York City Mayor John Lindsay, has made a number of recommendations that create opportunities for joint federal–municipal sponsorship of census-related research. See City of New York, Office of the Mayor, *The Report of the Mayor's Advisory Committee on the Census,* December 1970.

[13] An arrangement wherein the Bureau and an external research group agree to contribute relatively equal amounts of resources. The research contract and joint statistical agreement are the two instruments presently available to the Bureau for supporting external research. In order to make direct grants to individual researchers (dissertation fellowships, for example) the Bureau would have to work through another institution or seek a change in the Census Act.

research and training facilities in subject areas suggested by conceptions of the census as a social process. Such groups or institutions might be asked to undertake both short-term and long-term research projects, but the latter should be emphasized because of the special suitability of the university setting for exploratory research and training that is not directly linked to agency operating schedules.

A third possible approach would be to establish a program of support for dissertation research on problems of population enumeration and description. The advantages of such a program and some of the subject areas that it might cover are discussed in Chapter 4 (pp. 74–76). Alternatively, the Bureau might establish one program of its own and another jointly with other agencies that regard such research as a useful approach in dealing with their particular policy and program difficulties.

Fourth, it would be helpful if the Bureau would make a stronger effort to keep interested outside researchers informed of census-related studies either in progress or under consideration. In 1963, the Bureau established a Research Documentation Program to inform the Bureau staff of the status of ongoing research, to keep the staff abreast of related research being done by others, and to encourage wider external dissemination of Bureau research reports. The program compiles and publishes two annotated bibliographies. One, entitled *Quarterly Research Reports,* is intended primarily for circulation within the Bureau. The other, *Census Methodological Research: An Annotated List of Papers and Reports.*[14] is published annually. Despite the existence of annotated bibliographies, however, many people, including senior researchers, report great difficulty in threading their way through the history of census research on a problem like underenumeration.

It would also be useful for the Bureau to maintain and publish periodically a cumulative list of formal advice-giving and study-group activities that it sponsors, since such a listing would serve as a record of suggestions already accepted or rejected by the Bureau. However, at a minimum, the Bureau should make easily available a continuously updated bibliography of research projects, completed or in progress, so that outside researchers can keep informed of work that is still insufficiently developed to merit a published research report.[15]

[14] The most recent number is U.S. Bureau of the Census, *Census Methodological Research, 1970: An Annotated List of Papers and Reports* (Washington, D.C.: U.S. Government Printing Office), September 1971.

[15] As an illustration of one useful form that such a compilation might take, and also as a preliminary guide for interested researchers to what has been done on

Finally, the Bureau should explore the possibility of establishing an internship program, either independently or in cooperation with other interested agencies. This could help develop a broader awareness, both outside and inside government, of the operating requirements and constraints involved in collecting, disseminating, and using official social statistics. In particular, the Bureau should take advantage of opportunities to recruit, for one- or two-year appointments, young social scientists who have recently completed dissertations in new areas of census-taking research. In so doing, the Bureau would be investing both in the development of a new generation of needed researchers and facilitating changes in the present composition of its permanent research staff.[16]

In-House Research Capability   The extent to which even a well-articulated and substantially funded network of external research relationships can contribute to the improvement of census-data quality will depend on the capacity of the Bureau to translate research results into operational procedures and programs. At present, social scientists are not strongly represented in the Bureau. Statistical research by subject-matter specialists does occur; however, the idea of the census being a social process, or an instrument of social policy that in some measure shapes the future of the nation, is not the kind of perspective to which the professional staff of the Bureau appears to be adequately attuned by training or experience. Hence, future changes in or additions to the Bureau research and policy-making staffs should be made with a view to enhancing their capacity for building intellectual bridges that will promote constructive interchange of knowledge and experience between the Bureau and the research communities it wishes to attract.

In particular, the Bureau must be equipped to take full advantage of the theoretical and methodological developments that may emerge from the work of social scientists not usually regarded as engaged in

---

the undercount problem thus far, an annotated bibliography of published material on estimating the extent and components of census underenumeration is included in this report as Appendix C. The bibliography was prepared by the Advisory Committee's Subcommittee on Alternatives to the Census.

[16] The Census Bureau established a Center for Research in Measurement Methods in 1964 with goals very much like those recommended here, although with a more limited perspective with regard to supporting broadly based and conceived social research. The principal impediments to achieving the goals outlined above have been the limited resources available (about $200,000 per year) and perhaps also the Bureau's lack of grant-making authority.

research directly related to census-taking problems. This would require the Bureau both to recognize the potential relevance of unsolicited proposals coming from a variety of research communities and to engage in continuous, informal communication with researchers already at work on problems that had not been thought of as bearing on difficulties of census data collection and use. It means also that the Bureau staff will have to be familiar with behavioral and social science research supported by other government agencies and will have to be capable of making decisions with regard to the appropriateness of different kinds of institutional research capabilities—university, nonprofit, private-for-profit, state, municipal, or in-house—for meeting various aspects of the Bureau's research needs.

Most important, there should be continuous interaction between the development of social science knowledge, both internally and externally, and the development of operating programs, field tests, and experiments. In designing a controlled media experiment (see p. 83), for example, closer linkages between the activities of the Bureau's Office of Public Information and the principal preoccupations of the Census Research and Evaluation Program will help to assure that there is adequate understanding of the kind of variation that is important and the factors that must be held constant. Past attempts to improve census-data quality will also have to be examined carefully in the light of new research perspectives, so that the Bureau staff will be better able to define new knowledge needs and to initiate the steps necessary to assure that those needs are fulfilled.

To develop the internal social science competence that it needs, the Bureau will have to offer salaries that will be attractive to able and experienced individuals in the academic world, as well as opportunities for professional development. In many respects, the Bureau already maintains such an environment. It encourages its staff to play prominent roles in the relevant professional societies and to publish, independently, papers and reports based on internal research projects. However, in attempting to attract new kinds of research competence and to foster new research approaches, particular attention should be paid to questions of project continuity and staffing depth. Subject-matter specialists recruited to work, for example, on studies of the meaning of census terms, the dynamics of the interviewer–respondent relationship, the characteristics of addresses at which mail delivery is difficult, and the development of sets of socioeconomic variables associated with census-taking deficiencies[17]

---

[17] These examples refer to research recommendations in Chapter 5.

should be encouraged to pursue their research on a continuing basis. They should be given full access to the planning and evaluation work being done on a specific census, but they should not always be compelled to adapt their own research schedules to the operating schedule of the Bureau.

To assure such independence, changes may have to be made in the present pattern of research funding. Instead of a research budget that is calculated as a percentage of the cost of taking each decennial census, or one that is contingent on the estimated cost of planning and pretesting a forthcoming census, the Bureau should have funds for a continuing program of exploratory social and behavioral science research on census-taking difficulties. Since the present annual research and development budget is tailored to support of work of a statistical or methodological nature, the Bureau should anticipate the need for a sharp increase in its research budget to at least double the amount currently expended on research and development. Increments may also be required in the funds allotted for planning and pretesting the 1980 and proposed 1975 Censuses, as well as in the Bureau's annual appropriation for staff salaries.

An effort should be made, moreover, to recruit more than a skeleton staff of subject-matter specialists. The question of critical staff size will be affected by the decision-making level at which the knowledge and advice of new categories of social scientists is sought, but the Bureau's ability to attract competent people will also depend on the number and quality of behavioral and social scientists recruited and on the variety of disciplinary perspectives and training they represent.

Independent Advisory Relationships   In addition to developing a stronger social and behavioral science research capability, the Bureau will want to engage in a continuing dialogue with social scientists who are working or have worked in census-related fields but who, for one reason or another, are not presently engaged in research projects funded by the Bureau. One of the easiest ways to maintain such a dialogue would be to establish an independent social and behavioral science research advisory committee, charged with the task of evaluating the findings of research conducted in house or funded externally by the Bureau. Like the Panels of Statistical Consultants on which the Bureau has drawn for advice, such a committee should be a continuing body with oversight responsibilities broader than any specific set of research projects or any specific area of research inquiry. Members should be appointed for periods of two or three years and should be kept closely informed of all work being done by or for the Bureau from the initial stage of research design to the final evaluation of research findings.

If properly constituted and located, such a committee will help the Bureau to win broader recognition for its efforts to promote creative collaboration between methodological and subject-matter specialists. The opportunities for fruitful cooperative work on census-taking problems by social scientist and statistician together seem to be truly substantial. Statistical strength exists in the Bureau, as it has for many years. In a number of cases, that expertise, guided by substantive hypotheses, has made solid contributions to the solution of social survey problems. In the future, however, not only must the Bureau's statistical competence be maintained, but also steps should be taken to foster even more frequent and intimate collaboration with specialists in areas of the social sciences that can offer new insights and assistance in resolving important enumeration difficulties. For understanding a problem like underenumeration, statistical analyses and field experiments to ascertain whether one procedure counts more people, or elicits more information, than another are useful. Yet, whenever possible, such studies should be supplemented by other kinds of inquiries designed to develop hypotheses that explain more fully why it is that certain procedures are effective with particular categories of persons at certain times and under specific social conditions. With hypotheses about why—hypotheses that go well beyond anecdotal speculation—it should then be possible to design more efficient and informative field experiments.

4   The Social Psychology of Anonymity: A Research Perspective

A census is an organized human activity that attempts to count and describe the components of a population as they appear at particular points in time. Like most other tallies, therefore, census counts are produced through a series of interactions among counter and counted that take place amidst an ongoing flow of events and changing rela-· tionships into which the census-taking process periodically intrudes. A census is, in effect, a socially organized activity interposed among other socially organized activities, or patterns of human perception and behavior, that to varying degrees may enhance or reduce the possibility of achieving an accurate count.

The principal concern of this chapter is the research implications of four social–psychological features of census operations that can affect the accuracy of the resulting data: the purposes for which a census is taken; its underlying assumptions about the structure of social reality; the sensitivity of census counting instruments; and the dependence of the census on human behavior in a variety of situations that are both created by and independent of the enumeration process. The intent of the chapter is to broaden the perspective from which the activities of social data-gathering organizations are customarily viewed. Thus, it should be read less as a set of specific research recommendations than as a map of conceptual routes along which future research on underenumeration and related census problems would be wisely directed.

The central premise of the chapter is that "missing" people are not inherently missing, or invisible, or anonymous, until they are made so by a lack of fit between the assumptions and procedures that guide the counting operation that attempts to locate them and the subjective, experiential categories, or characteristic behaviors, in which they define their own life situations. The chapter emphasizes the fact that social data are not simply "out there for the asking," but rather are structured in terms of purposes, assumptions, instruments, and interactions among people, which to varying degrees perturb, focus, and depend on the customary ambits of everyday life.[1]

Purposes: Why the Census Counts What and How It Counts

An examination of the social–psychological contexts of census taking brings into focus a number of questions that touch upon the problem of fit between the image of social organization projected by a census and what it is that census users want or need to know about the structure of social reality. From a social–psychological point of view, one of the most important questions to ask about a census is whether some people are excluded from the counting universe because the various enumeration categories and procedures used simply do not comprehend the characteristic features of their daily lives. Indeed, it is conceivable that some portion, perhaps even a large one, of the census undercount (and of analogous misclassification and misreporting problems) can be traced to inadequate recognition in the census of the variety and complexity of human social experience.

For example, comparative data on migrant groups, both in the United States and abroad, suggest that the difficulty of contacting and describing people in central cities may be as much a function of the stress placed on residential attachments, the primary device for identifying people to be counted, as it is a consequence of the fact that the places where people live are sometimes situated in ghettos. The passage of migrants from rural regions into, through, and out of urban centers is often organized in terms of the extended family rather than the family residence or household (the latter being commonly associated, in the United States, with the concept of nuclear family). Hence, some people may be missed by the census for the simple reason that the attachments they maintain to one, albeit unusual, form of primary group (the extended family) confer upon

---

[1] The theoretical framework for much of the ensuing discussion is derived from such sources as Peter L. Berger and Thomas Luckmann, *Social Construction of Reality: A Treatise in the Sociology of Knowledge* (Toronto: Doubleday), 1966; Harold Garfinkel, *Studies in Ethnomethodology* (Englewood Cliffs: Prentice-Hall), 1967; and Aaron Cicourel, *Method and Measurement in Sociology* (Glencoe: The Free Press), 1964.

them social identities that make them unrecognizable as countable persons within the census framework of expected primary group linkages.

Further analysis of policy purposes in terms of the specific social information requirements they pose could lead to the identification of new counting units of a sort that would enhance the "social visibility" of people presently thought likely to be missed by the census. The practice of linking all individuals to residential units has historical roots in the first decennial census in 1790, when a modified version of the *de jure*[2] enumeration method was selected to achieve the principal purpose of the census at that time—apportionment of the Congress. Today, however, it seems advisable to ask whether the household still makes sense as the basic reporting unit for many present or anticipated uses of census data.

For example, if a policy objective were to assure that every individual adult has adequate means of support, a first question would be: Which population unit should such programs try to affect? The family? Individuals? Working-age males? Then, given that determination, the next question would be how best to collect needed information about those units—how many there are and their characteristics. In some cases, the appropriate reporting units may turn out to be households, but in others it could be such things as employers or school enrollments.

Careful attention to the degree of fit or lack of fit between what census users want to know and what the census tells them could lead in other useful directions as well. For the immediate future, it might further attest to the utility of gathering the same, different, or supplementary categories of social data at more frequent intervals. One aspect of present user difficulties is clearly the fact that census statistics fall short of representing the current state of the society because of the infrequency with which they are collected. Although the changing nature of social reality renders a census count inaccurate minutes after it is made, that degree of inaccuracy can, for most purposes, be ignored. If, however, it is important, for adminis-

---

[2] There are basically two approaches to census taking used throughout the world, both of which endeavor to obtain a count of bodies within some defined set of boundaries and to gather information about their social characteristics in the process. One approach is the so-called *de facto* census: a count of people where they are at a particular moment in time. The other is the *de jure* approach: an enumeration of individuals at their place of residence, even though they may not be in that place at the time the census is taken.

trative purposes, to chart the pattern of racial succession in one or more areas, and the data being used are eight, six, or even two years old, it is often questionable whether they can provide adequate information about the number and distribution of the individuals actually involved, no matter how accurate the counts may have been at the time they were made.

The objection can be made, of course, that collecting different or more timely bodies of social data will not reduce underenumeration *per se*, since the same kinds of people are likely to be uncounted in any survey. The premise of that objection need not hold, however, if undercounting is regarded as a serious problem only to the extent that it prevents functional information requirements from being met. In the case of information that serves the task of social problem definition, for example, underenumeration in the census is a significant impediment in two principal instances: if uncounted persons differ markedly from counted individuals, thereby distorting the overall image of the society projected by a census; and if uncounted persons contribute in some unique way to a specific problem that requires definition.

In the first case, the possibility that undercounted groups have peculiar characteristics that make them unusually and consistently difficult to enumerate in the decennial censuses and other social surveys is an obstacle that would not necessarily be surmounted by more frequent data-gathering efforts along the same lines as the census. In the second case, however, more frequent censuses or surveys, some of them perhaps designed to serve special purposes, could help to relieve present problems of data collection and interpretation. Gains could possibly be made by increasing the variety of cuts that are made into the social processes that warrant description for one or another public policy purpose.

Making a larger variety of incisions into particular sets of structured social relationships might, on one hand, increase the probability that persons in certain categories could be located and described, and, on the other, have the long-term effect of creating and reinforcing habits of responding to census and survey queries. Certainly, more frequent efforts could be expected to produce a more efficient census-taking organization and probably also a better-informed public. How much easier would it be to evaluate within-household coverage in the census if census counts could be checked against five independent surveys like the CPS? How much more light could such a multiplication of matching resources shed on the characteristics of persons thereby identified as having a high probability of being missed? How much more cooperative might undercounted groups be if they understood more fully the relevance of census or survey inquiries to their special problems?

These are obviously long-term research considerations. They clearly imply a vigorous role for the statistical agencies of government in determining the form and content of censuses and social surveys. But they do call attention to the fact that the relationship between policy purposes and a counting universe can be defined in different ways, thereby increasing or decreasing the probability that certain people will or will not be counted.

Theory: The Census Image of Social Reality

Counting operations characteristically begin with a more or less explicit conception of the underlying relationships among the phenomena they propose to locate and describe. In the American *de jure* census, the implicit theory of social organization that guides the design and execution of an enumeration posits a population arranged according to linkages individuals maintain to places of residence. That is, in the United States, a principal objective of the decennial censuses is to count people where they live. Moreover, for most of the population, it is expected that the place of residence will be a household.[3]

The counting framework for the decennial censuses thus resembles a two-dimensional grid. It is a scheme for grouping people in space. The intention is that each individual entity should be clearly visible and that no persons should be left floating in the interstices of the counting framework. Nomadism is a readily suspected source of counting error in such a context. Hence, intensive enumeration procedures—"T-night,"[4] mover checks, casual setting interviews,

[3] The persons in a housing unit constitute a household. For the 1970 population census, a housing unit was defined as a house, an apartment, a group of rooms, or a single room occupied or intended for occupancy as separate living quarters. Separate living quarters are those in which the occupants do not live and eat with any other persons in the structure and that have either direct access from the outside of the building or through a common hall or complete kitchen facilities for exclusive use of the occupants. See U.S. Bureau of the Census, *1970 Census of Housing*, "General Housing Characteristics—Advance Report," HC (6), February 1971, p. 2.

[4] A special enumeration of transients in hotels, motels, and other establishments having accommodations for at least 50 transient guests. It is conducted on

street-corner "Were you counted?" campaigns—tend to focus on persons in transit from one place to another.

Such a conception of how the society is organized has served the census well in the past. The ability to count and describe 97 percent of the population suggests widespread correspondence between the census counting grid and the associational reality of everyday life. However, close examination of the presumed residence–household arrangement as a primary mode of social linkage would seem to be warranted, in principle, by the present scale and intensity of geographic mobility within the society, by the fact that multiple residence is no longer uncommon, and by the possibility that new forms of primary association may be emerging that do not correspond to the census definitions of residence and household. Indeed, residence may eventually come to be defined within a relative framework, so that persons may designate different places as their residences, depending upon the context of the question asked, without any one place being regarded as a regular home.

Also, as suggested earlier, a very immediate and practical reason why the residence–household linkage merits examination is that some social action programs may be having difficulty reaching their target populations because they are guided by a statistical profile of the population that stresses the ties that people have to the places where they live. Logically, to ask, "Who is living or staying here and has no other home?" is to postulate that people have one primary household attachment that is more important to them than all others and that those uniquely important attachments are known to the respondents who actually fill out the census form or respond to a census interviewer.

There are several possible approaches to examining these questions. The basic query concerns the relationship between locatability and countability and the variability in that relationship, if any, that would qualify the presumed relationship between residence and social linkage.

One approach would be to look carefully, from a sociological

---

the night of March 31. Reports for persons who claim another residence elsewhere are then forwarded to the communities in which they usually live to be checked against schedules filled out by someone at the person's usual residence. Persons who do not claim usual residence elsewhere are included in the enumeration district in which they are found. See U.S. Bureau of the Census, *1960 Censuses of Population and Housing: Procedural History* (Washington, D.C.: U.S. Government Printing Office), 1966, p. 55.

point of view, at what is implied in the way in which the census operationally defines its basic concept of household. Is there some way to sharpen the concept? It may be useful, for instance, to discard the idea of a housing unit and think about each room as a potentially dividable living space.

Another approach would be to examine the different ways in which a person may be related to a household. There can be different kinds of "in and out" relationships with a household, or between two households. There may be a certain period of time in which some people will be out of touch with any given household. Sometimes they may divide their time between two. If so, it is conceivable that some different counting strategy is needed, perhaps one for estimating the characteristics of households that have such "in and out" relationships, so that, whenever a survey or a census is conducted, it will be possible to weight the counted components in a way that will produce an estimate of the number of people who happen to be missing at that time.

A third approach would be to undertake some exploratory investigation of what it is that makes a person achieve visibility in different social circumstances and in different counting and identification frameworks. One step in that direction would be to study location and identification efforts other than the census. How are people who are conventionally locatable in fact located? By name? By name and address? By telephone and mailing lists? What are the routinized, matter-of-course ways of communicating with people? What strategies are employed to find individuals for whom search mechanisms cannot be systematized? What methods used by private detectives, skip tracers, bill collectors, and epidemiologists are likely to yield useful insights into the degree of procedural flexibility that is required to find and identify certain kinds of persons?[5]

Finally, it would be useful to examine the present census image of social reality with a view to substituting a more fluid, "interactionist" view of the society. In its present form, the census conception of how

---

[5] See, for example, N. E. Wilcox, "Patient Follow-up Procedures, Techniques, and Devices for Improvement," *American Journal of Public Health and the Nation's Health*, 55, pp. 1741–1756; Eugene E. Levitt, "On Locating Closed Clinic Cases for Follow-up Study," *Mental Hygiene*, 42, 1958, pp. 89–93; and Dorothy Miller, Robert Barnhouse, Richard Fallenbaum, and William Dawson, "Skip Tracers, Investigators, and Social Scientists: Ethics and Problems of Techniques of Follow-up Studies" (San Francisco: Scientific Analysis Corporation), Unpublished, 1966.

American society is organized appears to be constructed on the basis of three premises. First, the theory posits what daily observation appears to confirm—that most people become known, or "socially visible," to one another in the context of established, well-articulated networks of human association, of which the household is a particular form. Second, it recognizes that those associational networks provide routine opportunities for people to draw attention to themselves—to hold themselves out, as it were, in anticipation of being sought. Third, the census conception of social reality appears to assume that the more elaborately and closely linked an individual is to associational networks in which commonplace forms of social organization predominate, the more readily he will be able to respond "correctly" to census queries. The expectation seems to be that, even when a question does not correspond exactly to the way an individual would normally describe certain features of his daily life, it will be easier for him to respond in a manner that satisfies the intentions of the query if the relationships that define his daily existence are relatively conventional and stable.[6]

This is not an unreasonable explanation of how human populations are organized and of how human behavior is patterned. Because most people have regular occupations, belong to churches and clubs, borrow money from banks, pay taxes, and vote, they can reasonably be expected to have a primary place of residence at a particular point in time, to put out mail boxes, to list themselves in a telephone directory, and to leave forwarding addresses when they move. For most, moreover, the family or kinship group is the most common identifying community. If a man wants to find another person, he will generally make inquiries among the sought person's relatives. Contacting the other's kin may not be the first step in his search, but it is a step that will surely be taken if others fail.

The census theory, however, does not adequately stress the fact that social structure is continually being renegotiated by people; that the underlying arrangements of society are not as stable and uniform as outward appearances might suggest. In looking, for instance, at some of the special census procedures that have been devised to count people in "unconventional" places, it is striking how readily

[6]See, for example, the discussion of this problem in Howard V. Stambler, "Problems of Analysis of Urban Employment Survey Data," *Proceedings of the Social Statistics Section of the American Statistical Association*, 1968, pp. 31–34.

attention is directed to the possibility of an individual—such as the itinerant derelict—being completely and permanently outside conventional societal networks. Less emphasis, however, is given to the possibility and consequences for counting of, say, isolation from conventional social institutions being but a stage in a career.

Individuals who are running from the law and those who have recently returned to the society from prisons or mental institutions are people who may have unusual but nonetheless observable attachments to certain kinds of social institutions, which, if better understood, would increase the likelihood that they could be found and described when wanted.

Similarly, the young person who today deliberately emancipates himself from commitments to family ties and inherited career patterns may or may not maintain that status for life. However, because he and others like him have yet to project into their lives images of predictable life patterns, they may for a time lack important linkages to networks of human association that would make clear, both to themselves and to others, the precise nature of their membership in one or more primary social groupings. What does living in a commune mean to a young person? Indeed, even in relatively conventional situations, it is not farfetched to imagine the ambiguities that might attend a man being the head of several households, the holder of several jobs, or a child being the dependent of several families.

The present census theory, in sum, seems to imply that there is a set of procedures that is adequate for counting most of the population, and that the remainder, which is relatively small and thought to be made up of people with unconventional social characteristics, requires more subtle procedures. In some instances, this may be an eminently sensible approach. Undoubtedly, there are individuals, such as the itinerant derelict, whose existence and identity can be determined only by tracing their physical movements from place to place. They are people who have multiple identities as a consequence of idiosyncratically organized movements that give them a different identity in each place they appear. No one person or group of persons is continuously informed about where they are, or who they are, were, or are becoming.

An interactionist view of the society, however, would suggest that such extreme cases should not be considered unconventional relative to some standard predicated for a majority of the population, but rather should be regarded as a category of individuals who function in segmented associations that are threaded in diverse patterns throughout the entire fabric of the society. In other words, an interactionist social theory would assert (a) that there are many different kinds of people to whom census expectations about conventional life styles may appear to diverge markedly from the subjective, experiential categories in which they define their life situations; (b) that there are categories of people who have decidedly less conventional life situations than others; but (c) that neither conventional nor unconventional expectations about the organization of people's lives may be applicable to the same people all the time. An interactionist theory would, in effect, place stronger emphasis on the fact that respondents in censuses and social surveys are not only constantly striving to make sense of the events and relationships that define their own daily lives, but that they also must interpret and answer survey queries in terms of their particular perceptions of those events and relationships at given moments in time.

The Counting Instrument: The Meaning of Census Inquiries and Their Sensitivity

Even if it were possible to determine the most efficient conceptual space for counting a population, the census would probably miss some theoretically countable individuals. The reason is that the effectiveness of any procedure for counting people, be it self-enumeration or having one individual report for others associated with a given reporting unit, is partially dependent on the degree to which it helps potentially countable persons to enhance or reduce their visibility to the outside world. In some cases, of course, errors in counting results will be traceable to purposeful, willfully evasive behavior, but in others they will be seen to arise from inadvertent oversight or simple misunderstanding.

From the point of view of survey research operations, the problematic dimensions of respondent behavior converge in questions about respondent ignorance, indifference, resistance, hostility, or rejection of specific efforts to induce them to participate cooperatively in enumeration and survey efforts. Here attention is initially confined to the first of these—namely, the perceptual aspects of the census counting operation that could occasion incomplete or inaccurate responses to the kinds of questions asked under census conditions.

For some individuals, there may be cultural, linguistic, or social obstacles that stand in the way of communicating the intended meaning of census queries. Consider the problem of deciding how many individuals are attached to a given household. What does it mean to ask: "Who was living here on April 1, 1970?" "Are there any other persons in this household?" or "Did anyone stay here on Tuesday, March 31, who is not already listed?" To ask such a question is to assume that communication is taking place, although there are no doubt some population subgroups (ethnic, socioeconomic, cultural) for whom the meaning of terms such as "living," "staying," "visiting," "household" do not have straightforward denotations. Are the differences in interpretation sufficient to cause the respondent in an otherwise enumerated household to interpret the census or another survey's definition of household member in a way that would cause him to omit someone who "should" be considered a part of his household? What does the concept of "living here" mean in the life styles of different kinds of people? What percentage of his time and under what circumstances (eating, sleeping) must a person spend in a household to be identified by other members as "living" or "staying" there?[7]

There are several existing bodies of knowledge that could provide insight into the variety and implications of perceptual problems raised by standard survey definitions. Sociologists, for example, have identified people for whom the relationship between household and fixed address is always extremely tenuous. Research on skid row derelicts has shown that restaurants, bars, and jails commonly serve as mail-drops, an observation that raises questions about the extent to which, even at prior stages of the enumeration process, perceptual problems—e.g., what does the mailman consider a valid address?—could exclude places or situations in which some people might consider themselves to "live" or "stay."[8] Observations have been made

[7] A number of demographic and social surveys in less developed countries have had to deal with considerable cultural variation along these lines. By systematic analysis of the operational definitions they used (in particular cultural contexts), useful light may be shed on analogous problems in the United States. A modest bibliography is provided by J. C. van Es and Eugene A. Wilkening in their article, "Response Stability in Survey Research: A Cross-Cultural Comparison," *Rural Sociology*, 35, June 1970. Other relevant items include National Family Planning Board, *Report on West Malaysian Family Survey* (Kuala Lumpur: Kim Printers), 1968; and The Population Council, Demographic Division, *Selected Questionnaires on Knowledge, Attitudes, and Practice of Family Planning* (New York: The Population Council), 1967.

[8] See, for example, Egon Bittner, "The Police on Skid Row: A Study of Peace Keeping," *American Sociological Review*, 32, October 1967, pp. 699–715; and Harold Garfinkel with the assistance of Egon Bittner, "Methodological Adequacy

of the manner in which differences in vocabulary and syntactical patterns affect the cues to which individuals attend in their everyday environments and the conclusions that they draw from given sets of premises. Studies have been made of the association between "correct" inferences and a number of possible meanings that individuals are prepared, by experience or formal instruction, to attribute to unfamiliar or ambiguous terms.[9]

Moreover, investigation of the meanings ascribed to standard survey terms and census identification categories should not be restricted to those used to elicit basic demographic information. While greater completeness and accuracy in the reporting of items such as income may not contribute directly to reducing the incidence of undercoverage, both the recognized need for more accurate and detailed data on certain subpopulations and the possible relationship between underenumeration and selective nonresponse to specific categories of survey questions seem to argue for inquiry into the perceived meanings of an array of key social data concepts.

Definitions of work and income are, for some people, extremely loose. Their sources of income are varied and often cannot be broken down into wages, salaries, commissions, and the like. Among ghetto residents, for example, information about income is not readily volunteered to anyone, and the census is, of course, not apt to be informed of income derived from illegal businesses or from welfare checks for which the recipient–respondent is legally ineligible. Opportunities to study the divergent meanings of "work," "education," and "income" thus suggest possibilities for fruitful exploration not only of the substantive interpretations accorded such usages, but also of the kinds of questions and the contexts in which respondents will not (because of inability or unwillingness) answer accurately or fully.[10]

---

in the Quantitative Study of Selection Criteria and Selection Activities in Psychiatric Outpatient Clinics," in Garfinkel, *op. cit.*, pp. 208–261.

[9] See, for example, William Labov, "The Logic of Nonstandard English," in Frederick Williams (Ed.), *Language and Poverty* (Chicago: Markham), 1970, pp. 153–189; and Michael Cole, John Gay, Joseph Glick, and Donald Sharp, *The Cultural Context of Learning and Thinking* (New York: Basic Books), 1971.

[10] See, for example, Aaron Cicourel, "Fertility, Family Planning and the Social Organization of Family Life: Some Methodological Issues," *Journal of Social Issues*, 23, October 1967, pp. 57–81.

A member of the Advisory Committee's Subcommittee on the Social Psychology of Anonymity once characterized this research problem as follows:

The Counting Process: Its Effects on Human Behavior

Research on political participation, and the inclination of individuals to engage in cooperative group activity generally, indicates that the performance of acts regarded as civic responsibilities is positively related to socioeconomic status. By analogy, it might be inferred (provided that being counted in a census is regarded as a civic duty) that the number of missing individuals in a society would decline naturally as wealth and education become more uniformly dispersed. It might be thought, for instance, that people who hold more stable jobs would be more likely to be familiar with statistical inquiries, to be in places that make them more easily enumerated, and to be sensitive to the need for census information. Further, it might be argued that the inclination to perform a civic duty, if being counted can be so regarded, will increase with an individual's ability to present himself to the outside world in conventionally acceptable ways. Obviously, however, to formulate such expectations is to run the risk of assuming too direct a connection between gross population characteristics, such as socioeconomic status, and the perceptions and motivations that inform human behavior in specific social contexts. In the census case, moreover, to so speculate is to remove from consideration a range of still unexamined events and behaviors associated with the detailed process of counting people.

Not every citizen is eligible to vote. An election can take place even if only a small percentage of those who are eligible go to the polls. A census, however, requires both extensive population involvement and intensive participation on the part of those who actually complete the questionnaire. Furthermore, to take a census is to interpose a set of patterned human behaviors among other independently organized human activities. Hence, to understand a phenomenon such as census underenumeration, it is necessary to clarify in detail the relationship between external influences being exerted upon respondents at the time they decide whether or not they will permit themselves to be enumerated and specific inducements to cooperate, such as the behavior of census-taking personnel.

One useful approach to both categories of problems would be to

---

The census questionnaire asks if you have a flush toilet. I imagine that many respondents attempt to answer questions like that, even though they know that their situation does not quite correspond to the answer they must give. If I have a flush toilet, but it hardly ever works, so I have to get a bucket, do I or do I not have a flush toilet? Research is needed on how people understand such questions, and the kinds of interpretive processes that go on in these situations.

think of potential respondents as if arrayed along a continuum rang-
ing from willful evasion, misrepresentation, and inadvertent failure to
respond, through simple countability (with varying degrees of response
completeness), to complete, accurate reporting of all data. The advantage of such a framework is that it would identify some people
who do respond adequately to a request for information about themselves as having been potential nonrespondents, and would, therefore,
direct attention to the circumstances affecting their willingness to
cooperate. Further, it would have the advantage of suggesting an interesting range of intermediate cases, as well as alternative research
and ameliorative approaches to different combinations of problems
manifested at different points along the continuum.

Another approach would be to look directly at the effect on respondent behavior of such factors as group membership, fear of the
consequences of a complete, accurate response, and subtle aspects of
enumerator comportment or attitudes, which may adversely impinge
upon the quality of census results. Studies of political behavior, for
example, indicate that primary group relationships are to some extent predictive of voting choices; that the performance of one civic
duty, voting, is related to subjective assessments of personal competence; and that, as mentioned earlier, a person's confidence in his
ability to affect policy outcomes through civic action is related, at
least in the United States, to socioeconomic status and its attendant
forms of primary group membership. Hence, it would seem useful to
inquire into the circumstances surrounding the motivation to comply
voluntarily with an official request to provide information about
oneself and others, in order to determine the nature of influences
forthcoming from the primary group, the role played by subjective
assessments of the efficacy of compliance, and the relationship of
those assessments to factors such as income, education, and social
status.

Along the same lines, it is important to understand the impact of
external networks of communication on the extent of respondent
compliance or noncompliance. What roles do organizational membership and relationships to community authority structures play in the
receptivity of people to survey publicity? How effective are community leaders as mediators of promises of data confidentiality? Which
components of interpersonal trust, group loyalty, and choice behavior make appeals through organized groups more or less effective than
requests directly to individuals? What efforts do people make to get
themselves counted as "members" of political parties and social clubs,

or to keep their names on subscription lists? Ideological resistance to being counted should also be studied in connection with group allegiances. Whether or not resistant and negative attitudes toward polling activities of all kinds are becoming more frequent is an empirical question whose social and behavioral dimensions deserve systematic investigation.

Similarly, attention should be given to the anxiety that survey queries, or knowledge that a survey is being taken, might induce in some respondents. Using the mail means that people hold themselves out, as it were, to be found. They put out mailboxes with numbers and thus ease the task of the mailman. Others, who do not do that, not only do not get mail, but probably also do not receive many other things. They may never be contacted by anyone outside their immediate circle and, hence, may wonder why they should make a special effort for the census. Most people probably fill out forms like the census schedule, or respond to the census-taker, because their place in the world depends upon doing "the right thing." They do not wish to tamper with that network of trust. For some people, however, there is simply no good in the system, and hence they feel no obligation to cooperate with it. How frequent or how latent or manifest is the fear that no good can come of volunteering for any public activity? Under what circumstances can such fears be dispelled or counteracted?

Still other individuals have very specific reasons for wanting to remain anonymous. In urban slums and tenements, there are people whose existence and whereabouts will not be acknowledged by anyone. Some are people whose admitted presence in the household would cause the loss of welfare eligibility or unemployment benefits. Others are garnishees or bankrupts or people involved in criminal activities. Some are people who fear violent death or injury at the hands of persons who have grievances against them.

Even more frequent, perhaps, are those who are reluctant to reveal information about themselves for fear of the invidious judgments that the information will provoke. They are people who have more poverty to hide, more ignorance, more joblessness, more illegitimacy—more of all the characteristics that make any probe into their life circumstances a threat to their self-respect. There are, for example, many poorly educated people who are terrified of the printed word, and their anxiety may not be greatly reduced by watching someone else complete a form for them.

An understanding of these patterns of reticence will reveal one large body of circumstances that condition the census-taking experience of some population subgroups. It will, however, reveal only one part. As a recent critic of the census has observed:

The question "Who are people?" is answered at the most fundamental level by the actual enumerator. If the customs and attitudes of a people allow an enumerator, consciously or unconsciously, to say, "What difference does one Negro more or less make?" or one Indian . . . then there *cannot* be a complete enumeration.[11]

Over the years, the Census Bureau has paid close attention to the possibilities for error occasioned by its counting procedures—the rules for coding and processing, the standards for selecting and training enumerators. The Bureau has also repeatedly measured the enumerator contribution to reporting inaccuracy—a principal reason why self-enumeration is now being used extensively—and has recently begun to conduct detailed studies of interviewing behavior in social surveys.[12] To date, however, the Bureau has not looked hard enough at the effects on the counting process of the attitudes and perceptions that enumerators bring to the census-taking task.[13]

What are the consequences of, say, an enumerator's distaste for dealing with people of a lower social class than his own? Of his or her fear of violence, or of dark, dirty places? It is difficult to imagine many enumerators going into an apartment house, or a three- or four-story building, if they have to walk up unlighted stairs littered with old whiskey bottles and other kinds of human waste. Some enumerators, of course, do perform follow-up work under such conditions, but some may not, and an effort should be made to measure and to discover how to compensate for such patterned evasion of census procedures.

Moreover, the process by which census field personnel are selected is an important aspect of census taking, which, to the Advisory Com-

[11] Hyman Alterman, *Counting People: The Census in History* (New York: Harcourt, Brace & World), 1969, p. 287.

[12] See, for example, National Center for Health Statistics, "The Influence of Interviewer and Respondent Psychological and Behavioral Variables on the Reporting in Household Interviews," *Vital and Health Statistics*, Public Health Service Publication No. 1000, Series 2, No. 26 (Washington, D.C.: U.S. Government Printing Office), March 1968.

[13] An important study in this area is summarized in Robert H. Hanson and Eli S. Marks, "Influence of the Interviewer on the Accuracy of Survey Results," *Journal of the American Statistical Association*, September 1958, 53, pp. 635–655.

mittee's knowledge, has not been examined thoroughly, and ought to be, given its conceivable contribution to a variety of census problems. Every census enumerator must pass a qualifying examination before being hired. In 1970, the "selection-aid" tests were designed to stimulate recruitment of residents of "intensive enumeration" areas, in particular, and members of minority groups, more generally. The tests are said, for example, to have stressed learning ability more than formal education, and in some places plans were made (but not implemented) to administer the tests in Spanish. In many areas of the country, however, applicants for the qualifying examinations were initially recruited by the traditional census referral system, which, in the opinion of many observers, places undue weight on the candidate's political affiliations.

More striking still is the number of field office supervisory positions that continue to be filled by patronage appointees, a practice that, critics of census operations contend, introduces subtle preselective factors into the manner in which many potential enumerators find out about the qualifying examinations and present themselves to take them.[14] One critical observer asserts, for example, that the referral system, "in wide areas of the country, leads to the exclusion of the Negro as an enumerator." It also, he alleges, accounts for the fact that in recent years most of the enumerators have been retired people and housewives, to whom "the country owes . . . a debt of gratitude for performing a difficult job with little reward," but who, "by the routine of their daily lives, are usually more withdrawn from the give and take of American life," and "more likely than others to be frightened by the ghetto way of life."[15]

It is generally thought that the hiring procedures followed in the intensive enumeration areas in 1970 lessened the likelihood of discordant contact between enumerators and respondents of widely different backgrounds and ages. In fairness to the Census Bureau, it should also be noted that, where large numbers of enumerators have been recruited without passing through the referral system, the enu-

---

[14] See, for example, testimony given by the late Whitney M. Young in U.S. Congress, House of Representatives, Subcommittee on Census and Statistics of the Committee on Post Office and Civil Service, *Hearings on the Accuracy of 1970 Census Enumeration and Related Matters*, 91st Congress, 2d Session (Washington, D.C.: U.S. Government Printing Office), September 1970, pp. 83–114.

[15] Alterman, *op. cit.*, pp. 288–289. See also *1960 Censuses of Population and Housing: Procedural History*, *op. cit.*, p. 43.

merator turnover rate has often been so high as possibly to offset whatever advantages might be expected to flow from a more impartial recruitment procedure. Yet such mitigating observations should not be permitted to obscure the essential point—namely, that the system, whatever its merits or defects, has been too little discussed in Census Bureau research and field reports.

An Agenda for Research on Social–Psychological Problems of Census Taking

As indicated at the outset, the intent of this discussion of census-taking purposes, concepts, procedures, and situations is to delineate the principal concerns of a long-term program of research and experimentation aimed at providing a continuous series of opportunities to reassess the Census Bureau's grasp of the complexities of the activities in which social data-gathering organizations engage. However, the present chapter does not purport to be a comprehensive listing of every aspect of census taking that may bear examination in social-psychological terms, nor do the more specific research recommendations in Chapter 5 exhaust the range of research possibilities indicated by consideration of the census as an interactive social process. Rather, what seems desirable at this juncture is a stronger commitment on the part of the sponsors of census and census-related research to continuing study of the social and social–psychological dimensions of population enumeration and description.

For example, studies should be encouraged in the following areas:

• Modes of social linkage within and among various social groups or categories and the effect of those linkages on social visibility, including studies of the ability of "insiders" to locate persons in such groups or categories

• Social organization and differentiation by life style, with particular emphasis on the effects of geographic and social mobility

• The relationship between life styles, life cycles, and conventional linkages to social institutions, including the role of ideologies in the maintenance or attenuation of such linkages

• The relationship between census and other standard demographic categories (for example, marital status, number of offspring, race, relationship to head of household) and the subjective categories used by members of specific subpopulations, such as ethnic subcultures, social dropouts, religious cults, and migrants and other marginal occupational groups

- Factors influencing decisions to participate or not to participate in sample surveys, including detailed analyses of the characteristics of dropouts from panel and list samples and from longitudinal and epidemiological studies
- The social bases, rationales, and consequences of ideological and related forms of doctrinal opposition to aggregate information-gathering by government and other public agencies
- Search methods of organizations routinely engaged in service or research activities that entail the location of "hard-to-find" populations—for example, welfare organizations, collection and credit agencies, market research operations that survey mobile populations, and organizations that compile registries of noncareer professionals, such as nurses, schoolteachers, and technicians

In addition, secondary analyses should be undertaken of social and behavioral science research findings related to the participation and compliance of populations in both voluntary and legally sanctioned governmental information-gathering activities (the Current Population Survey; public health surveys; municipal, state, and federal tax returns; various licensing and registration programs), as well as of internal Census Bureau reports and documents bearing on problems of resistance, hostility, refusal, or other cases of inadequate response to census queries.

Such a broad approach to census-taking problems has the disadvantage of diffuse formulation, but it offers the important benefit of suggesting many opportunities to develop new perspectives and conceptual frameworks for the exploration of phenomena not usually associated with social data deficiencies. Moreover, adopting an exploratory strategy that subjects the entire census-taking activity to a very broad critical examination and analysis is one of the best ways of enlisting the interest and cooperation of competent researchers who have not previously worked directly on census problems.

As suggested in Chapter 3 (p. 49), there are several ways in which the Census Bureau and other research sponsors interested in these problems might proceed toward developing the kind of research competence that would guarantee adequate, continuing attention to the social and social–psychological dimensions of the census-taking process. One way would be to establish a program of direct support for dissertation research on the social–psychological problems of population enumeration and description. By interesting young people in these sometimes exotic problems at early stages in their careers, the census could acquire a new, more broadly based research constituency inexpensively and within a relatively brief period of time. Another way would be to provide incentives to senior researchers either to work independently on such problems or to undertake projects that would include, in addition to their own work, sponsorship of one or more doctoral dissertations. Whatever organizing approach is chosen, however, the point to be emphasized is that there are already many excellent people working on questions raised in the foregoing discussion, and an effort should, therefore, be made to clarify the linkages between their substantive research interests and the knowledge needs of data-gathering organizations.

5   Anonymity in the Census Context: Specific Recommendations for Research

A number of ideas suggested by the conceptualization of census taking as a socially organized activity can be translated directly into research proposals aimed at improving standard enumeration procedures. Others require longer-term exploratory studies to develop additional evidence about the kinds of people who do not get counted, and how, and why. The recommendations that follow encompass research of both kinds. There are projects that could be undertaken as part of a relatively short-term census research and evaluation program, but there are also others, such as ethnographic and longitudinal studies of "hard-to-enumerate" populations, that will require both relatively longer periods of time and closer cooperation among the many potential sponsors and performers of research with implications for census and social survey operations.

In considering the various kinds of studies suggested, it will become apparent that the research questions raised tend to be but one step, albeit a large step, removed from the types of census-taking problems that have been addressed, often with singular success, in the past. Six of the areas in which recommendations are made—questionnaire design, personnel recruitment and training, design and dissemination of public information materials, scheduling, Post Office participation, and interviewing techniques—have already been subjected to intensive study. Two others, registration systems and record matching, have been areas of continuing interest. Indeed, only the ethnographic, longitudinal, and casual-interview proposals might be viewed as exceptions to the traditional style of research on census-taking problems, but, as indicated in previous chapters, even they have recent precedents.

In sum, the recommendations made here do not constitute a radical departure from past research approaches so much as a reorientation toward more explicit concern with the social contexts in which censuses and social surveys are conducted. It is frequently argued, for example, that undefined aspects of the census, usually referred to as "census conditions," make the decennial enumerations easier to complete than other social surveys. But the precise nature of those conditions, and the extent to which they arise out of circumstances directly created by the census, are not clearly understood.

Another way of increasing the amount of attention given to social aspects of the enumeration process would, of course, be to return to earlier research and evaluation studies in search of insights and explanations as to why some procedures may have been more effective than others. Certainly that line of inquiry should also be pursued. However, secondary analysis of findings produced with other research objectives in mind will not alone be sufficient. New projects will have to be initiated and new programmatic research commitments made in order to enlarge the variety of reasonable hypotheses and corroborative sources of information about the social dynamics of large-scale data-gathering efforts.

Questionnaire Design

Efforts to devise census and social survey questions and questionnaire formats that maximize the ability and willingness of respondents to provide complete and accurate information should continue to be encouraged and strengthened. The census population count and sample questionnaires, as presently designed, facilitate rapid data processing, but clarity and comprehensibility still ought to be viewed as goals that should not be readily sacrificed in the interest of rapid data dissemination.

Further, although more complete and accurate census returns may not contribute directly to improving census coverage, it seems advisable to continue to explore the implications for questionnaire design of the frequently hypothesized relationship between underenumeration and inaccurate or incomplete responses to certain categories of census and social survey queries. As suggested in Chapter 4 (pp. 66–68), there may be among some socioeconomic groups shared perceptions of, for example, "marital status," and "relationship to head" that would lead to excluding from the list of household members persons who, from the census point of view, should not be excluded. Given the many known varieties of family structure, does the observation that someone "lives here" mean that a person "sleeps here," "eats here," or "collects his mail here"? Does "relationship to the household head" signify a relationship to a specific person in a specific household or to an individual in a large and variously ramified kinship network?

At present, the experimental goal of planned work on alternative questions and questionnaire formats is too narrow. Rather than limiting the research objective to developing aggregate measures of the effectiveness of prototype schedules, questionnaire experiments should encompass systematic exploration of the social components of response variance. That is, *additional controlled experimental studies of questionnaire wordings and formats should be used (a) to investigate further the influence on response patterns of such factors as race, sex, age, region, and social class; (b) to explore respondent interpretations of alternative renderings of census terms; and (c) to assess the advantages of translating entire questionnaires into other languages.*

For example, systematic variation of questionnaires administered within and across subsamples drawn from populations that are relatively homogeneous by race and social class would provide useful information about race- and class-related patterns of respondent cooperation, meaning perception, term definition, and the like. Suppose that such a study indicated that, under the conditions of a particular survey, respondents with characteristics *x, y,* and *z* would often misreport information in questions 2, 5, and 12, while people with characteristics *a, b,* and *c* would frequently not respond to queries 1, 4, and 6. Such evidence would not shed direct light on the hypothesized relationship between within-household undercounting and other kinds of inaccurate or incomplete reporting, but it would promote understanding of the circumstances in which incomplete or false reporting occurs.

Finally, although the two-stage enumeration procedure used in the 1960 Census constituted a test of earlier proposals to collect the census head count and sample information separately, that experience should be examined more fully, and further tests of the two-stage procedure should be made in ghetto areas using simplified questionnaires that are tailored to ghetto perceptions and circumstances.

Personnel Recruitment and Training

Census enumerators generally appear to be far more effective in completing interviews than the interviewers of other survey organizations.

However, there are reasons to suspect that fear, mistrust, and resistance to being counted are growing in the nation's ghettos. There is also some evidence that the race of the interviewer is not a crucial determinant of that mistrust. Black researchers and interviewers from both public and private research organizations report meeting the same kind of resistance in black ghettos as do white researchers. The Census Bureau experience with indigenous enumerators in Philadelphia in 1967 similarly suggests that black enumerators are no better at census taking than their white counterparts. The problem is highlighted by enumerator turnover in ghetto areas during the 1970 Census. It is reported that in Harlem more than 600 enumerators were necessary to complete the census, although only 370 had initially been thought necessary to do the job.[1] Like experiences have been recorded in Washington, D.C., and many other cities.

In view of these disheartening results, it would nonetheless be advisable to make even stronger efforts to recruit indigenous personnel for census taking in ghetto areas. One reason is the apparent lack of practical alternatives, but it should also be emphasized that the ways in which local people might be most effectively employed in a census have yet to be exhaustively examined.

The difficulties in Philadelphia, in 1967, seemed to center on the fact that black enumerators were no more able than white enumerators to elicit accurate reports of the number of persons attached to contactable households. But it is also possible that, generally, those blacks who would be attracted to and qualified for the job of census enumerator might tend to be seen as white men in blackface by the people they are trying to count, or that an enumerator's standing in the community he is counting is as important as his race and residence.[2] In Harlem, and elsewhere, it is generally accepted that citizen

---

[1] The *New York Times*, August 1, 1970. Similarly high turnover rates were also experienced in the Urban Employment Surveys (UES), even though the interviewing staff, for the most part, worked full-time on the survey and lived in the neighborhoods being studied. One Census Bureau staff member has suggested four reasons why UES interviewers were difficult to retain: competing opportunities in the job market; lack of the skills required for adequate performance; inability to work independently—to set their own work schedules; and "reluctance to be exposed continuously to the crime problem in poverty neighborhoods." Earle J. Gerson, "Methodological and Interviewing Problems in Household Surveys of Employment Problems in Urban Poverty Neighborhoods," *Proceedings of the Social Statistics Section of the American Statistical Association*, 1969, p. 22.

[2] "In connection with a special census of the city of New York in 1957, neighborhood leaders were tested as [recheck] enumerators. The distinction

response to the 1970 Census would have been far lower had it not been for the public sanction given the enumeration by such groups as the Urban League and the NAACP, which are known and trusted by community residents.

In any event, *an effort should be made to ascertain the usefulness of providing indigenous enumerators with an identity other than that of agents of the Census Bureau.* A special city census, or a survey undertaken for another government agency, might provide an opportunity to experiment with, for example, subcontracting the follow-up enumeration task in several ghetto areas to local community action groups or youth groups. Although the contracting organization would legally be the agency of the Census Bureau, each participating member could also take the census oath.

The logic of such an experiment would hold that the interposition of a local organization between the community and the Census Bureau might diminish respondent fear and mistrust. Perhaps more important, it would postulate that the interposition of a familiar intermediary between the individual enumerator and the Census Bureau could enhance enumerator morale and commitment. Compared with the enumerator hired directly by the Bureau, the enumerator from the local contracting organization might see himself as a member of a collectivity rather than as someone who stands in a personal and fragile one-to-one relationship with a government agency. As such, and unlike his directly hired counterpart, he would, therefore, be better able to benefit from peer encouragement and assistance in carrying out his tasks.

Finally, *additional attention should be given to the feasibility of hiring mailmen as follow-up enumerators.* In a later section of this chapter (pp. 86–88), further study of the ways in which mail delivery procedures might affect the census is urged. Here, in contrast,

---

sought was between leaders and other residents, not between neighborhood and outside enumerators. ... Comparisons between their results and the original enumeration indicated that the recheck enumerators missed more persons than the original enumerators had." Leon Pritzker and N. D. Rothwell, "Procedural Difficulties in Taking Past Censuses in Predominantly Negro, Puerto Rican, and Mexican Areas," in David M. Heer (Ed.), *Social Statistics and the City* (Cambridge, Massachusetts: Harvard University Press for the Joint Center for Urban Studies of the Massachusetts Institute of Technology and Harvard University), 1968, pp. 73–74. This experience may be viewed by some as evidence that the Advisory Committee's proposal is not likely to succeed, but attention should be given to the changed relationship between black community leaders and their constituencies over the last ten or fifteen years. The situation in the ghettos in 1957 was probably far different from the situation today.

the concern is with the follow-up enumeration task to which mail-men may be especially well suited. They are not typically targets of hostility; they know the people in their delivery areas and are known by them; they are highly visible and easily identified by their uni-forms; and they are, as a group, highly literate. Alternatively, mail-men might be employed as assistants in filling out the census ques-tionnaire at the time of delivery, or at an agreed-upon time several days later, or they could be made responsible for having a member of a local volunteer corps do so.

Public Information Materials

It is useful to think of communication as a process involving (a) an event, (b) described and explained in messages, (c) that are trans-mitted through media, (d) to some audience, (e) that responds to them. When viewed as a communication problem, incomplete census or survey coverage may indicate that at least some of the intended respondents are inadequately informed about the event taking place and that the communication failure can be largely attributed to in-adequacies at steps (b) and (c).

In September 1969, the Advisory Committee's Subcommittee on Experimental Uses of the Census Public Information Campaign re-viewed the 1970 Census public information effort. From a communi-cation research point of view, several inadequacies were noted.

First, little information was available on levels of public knowl-edge about the census (the reasons for taking a census) or on public attitudes toward censuses, in particular, and social surveys, more gen-erally. Second, advertising and promotional materials were not pre-tested to determine their likely effect. As in previous census years, the advertising phase of the 1970 enumeration had been placed in the hands of a volunteer advertising group.[3] Hence, although the Census Bureau received welcome and useful professional assistance in preparing the 1970 public information campaign, it lost a large mea-sure of control over a crucially important aspect of the total census preparatory effort. Third, no systematic attempt was made to deter-mine the extent to which the prepared advertising or promotional materials were actually used by the mass media. And, fourth, no ef-

[3] The Advertising Council, Inc., of New York, which, in turn, assigned the actual task of preparing advertisements and media materials to one of its mem-ber agencies.

of the deaths of John and Robert Kennedy and Martin
ing might be considered, because of their special significance
oung, the poor, and racial minorities.

ce Cooperation and Mail Delivery Arrangements

*ould be continuing study of the perceptions and decision-
riteria that inform the editing of address registers by postal
is well as additional, more intensive, efforts to identify and
the characteristics of persons who allegedly live at addresses
mailmen find postal delivery especially difficult.*

liance of the 1970 Census on the postal service for assistance
fying and delivering census questionnaires to occupied dwell-
, as well as the possible advantages to be gained from ex-
the scope of the census by mail, suggests the importance of
ting in detail some of the processes involved in Post Office
tion. Two phases of census-related postal operations seem es-
worthy of study. One is the decision-making process by
dividual mailmen edit the address registers on which the cen-
ail depends. The other is the process by which mail is deliv-
people who presumably reside at addresses listed on the
.

regard to the first, it appears from Census Bureau studies of
ity of postal carriers to compile and edit an address register
ne dwelling units do not get listed on a register because of
ceptions commonly held by mailmen as to what constitutes a
dress. Vacant buildings slated for destruction in areas under-
rban renewal, abandoned automobiles on vacant lots, mobile
trucks, and other unconventional living spaces provide regular
for some segments of the population. Yet, if mailmen do not
uch unconventional dwelling places as legitimate addresses,
aces where people actually live, their occupants could well be
by a census.

tional investigation of how mailmen decide to include or ex-
welling units from the address registers they edit should pro-
dence of whether or not the hypothesis that residents of un-
tional places have a high probability of being missed is worth
g further. How, for example, do postmen decide that an ad-
nonexistent, or that a previously unlisted address should be
to the register? What are the characteristics of such addresses?
it that they do not appear on the original address register?

fort was made to determine the actual effect of the communication
campaign. Did it in fact help to improve census coverage?

Subsequently, in May 1970, a second subcommittee, the Subcommittee on Alternative Instruments for Improving Census Coverage,
attempted to translate the findings of the earlier group into recommendations for continuing research. Its recommendations were the
following:

1. *That a nationwide study of attitudes toward privacy and anonymity be conducted.* A baseline study of attitudes affecting compliance and noncompliance with official requests for information
would be a useful undertaking in its own right. The "privacy issue"
arises repeatedly in discussions of the census, of data banks, of computerized record systems, and of many other kinds of data collection
activities. Yet, there is still scant empirical evidence on which to base
judgments about public reaction to such developments (including
public understanding of the issues involved), nor is there adequate information about the consistency of public attitudes toward privacy
issues over time.

The proposed study would thus have two purposes. It would establish a baseline from which to measure future changes in public attitudes toward privacy and anonymity generally. It would also provide information about the characteristics of reluctant respondents,
from which, by extrapolation, hypotheses might be advanced about
the characteristics of people who do not respond at all.

2. *That a survey be made to gain a better understanding of how
the census is perceived.* The purpose of such a study would be to ascertain both the perceptions of the census that people entertain and
the motivations, events, or circumstances that encourage them to
answer, evade, or resist census inquiries. Conceptually, the study
would supplement a national survey of attitudes toward privacy and
anonymity by measuring attitudes and apparent respondent cooperation or resistance to one particular set of official queries. Ideally,
such a study should be undertaken at a time shortly before or after a
census—the proposed 1975 Census, for example—but it need not be
related to a national enumeration.

3. *That census public information material and media be thoroughly pretested.* All census advertising should be pretested, as a
matter of course, but special tests should be made with samples of
respondents of different age, sex, and race drawn from areas in
which the incidence of underenumeration is thought to be high.

Such studies might be done on a contract basis by the research department of an advertising agency. The object of pretesting, which should include some group interviews, would be to assess the general intelligibility and interest level of the materials and to detect any possible negative effects on respondent understanding of or disposition toward the census.

4. *That a content analysis be made of the national media effort.* The Census Bureau should be able to tell not only which informational and advertising materials were distributed to whom, but where, when, and how specific items (as well as census-related materials prepared by others) appeared in newspapers, magazines, and on radio and television. In particular, the presence or absence of the principal themes of a campaign should be noted, as well as regional variations in their popularity. The appearance of census materials in media most likely to reach potentially underenumerated groups should be the subject of a special follow-up analysis.

5. *That the effects of the public information campaigns be carefully evaluated.* It is essential that an evaluation of information procedures be included in any research undertaken in connection with a census. Specifically, pre–post sample surveys should be undertaken in several communities to determine, for each person interviewed, (a) his *awareness* of major information campaign themes and facts, (b) changes in his *attitude* toward the census (especially reinforcing or negative effects) that can be attributed to his exposure to one or more components of the information campaign, and (c) the *effects* of varying degrees of media saturation normally occurring and experimentally induced by selective purchase of media advertising.

6. *That funds provided for research to improve the census public information effort be sufficient to permit purchase of advertising.* Evaluation of the various communication strategies adopted by the Census Bureau should be done by an outside, independent agency that has not been involved in preparing the instrument or process being evaluated. Moreover, if other kinds of census-related research produce evidence that undercoverage is concentrated among narrowly defined social or ethnic groups, the Bureau will probably want to engage the services of advertising agencies that have had previous experience in preparing special media campaigns for such groups. Hence, it is important that funds be available for purchasing advertising and advertising services when needed.

In summary, *the utility of communication research as an instrument for gaining a better understanding of the reasons for census and*

---

survey undercoverage should be fully postcensal evaluation of the decennia campaigns is one important step, but study of attitudes toward privacy and can contribute more broadly to ident causes of census undercounting. In th progress is more likely to be made if a is developed between the Census Bure tion and the Census Research and Eva operative relationship should be of sul ties, inasmuch as the Information Offi experiment that, in 1970, was valued a

Census Scheduling

Enumeration dates other than April 1 s sidered. While there appears to be no c currences as the end of school terms, th and fluctuations in the need for seasona *further study of the effects of calendar- taking process.* At a minimum, the diffi rent Population Survey interviewers sho they exhibit seasonal differences, and th suses should be studied to see if there ar difficulty of contacting respondents and merators can be hired. The Committee h Bureau proposal, subsequently discarded sus in late April or in May, when follow-u had an additional daylight hour (because which to contact households—particularl was at home on initial visits.

In addition, it would be useful to exam that might be made by linking the census national holiday, or to an informally mark memorates some nationally significant eve ample, offers the triple advantage of heigh regular occurrence on the same day of the tional association with holiday travel and v

[4] In 1960, the estimated figure was $6 million.
1960 Censuses of Population and Housing: Proced D.C.: U.S. Government Printing Office), 1966, p.

least appear so to a census taker with standard and therefore limited persuasive resources at his disposal.

It may be, however, that information provided by enumerators about the nature of the census and its purposes and requirements could allay a respondent's fear, sense of alienation, or hostility. There is reason to think that public acceptance and cooperation is generally greater in the census than in other survey activities. Moreover, it has been a general policy of survey researchers to provide respondents with the minimum information needed to orient them properly to the questions that follow. Part of the reason has been a belief that, even if interviewers could be expected to understand all the purposes to which the collected information would be put, they might bias answers by the manner in which they ask the questions. Yet there are, no doubt, certain categories of potential respondents who do not believe that the answers they are asked to supply will result in benefits to them. Sometimes they may even believe that disclosing such facts about themselves and others will lead to injury.

In order to learn more about the reasons for respondent reticence, as well as about the relationship between explanatory information and respondent cooperation, experiments should be conducted in which the respondents in follow-up interviews are given different levels of information about the inquiries being made. For example, one group of respondents might be given the information commonly given in the Current Population Survey; another, more detailed explanations than in the CPS, including printed information and samples of how the resulting statistics appear in publication; and a third, illustrations of how data collected in the interview are to be used.

In addition, there is a need for more research on interviewer expectations and the manner in which they affect the data elicited. A recent evaluation of the Health Interview Survey, undertaken jointly by the Census Bureau and the National Center for Health Statistics, found reason to expect that the quality of the information produced in a survey interview depends more on the amount of behavioral interaction between respondent and interviewer than on the precision with which the questioning rules are followed.[8] Thus, it seems important to ask how typical interviewers and respondents conceive of

[8] National Center for Health Statistics, "The Influence of Interviewer and Respondent Psychological and Behavioral Variables on the Reporting in Household Interviews," *Vital and Health Statistics*, Public Health Service Publication No. 1000–Series 2, No. 26 (Washington, D.C.: U.S. Government Printing Office), March 1968, p. 35.

one another—not only what each "understands" by the other's question and response, but also what kinds of discounting, unwitting accommodation, and semantic distortion take place between the two with respect to key data collection categories.

However difficult such projects may be, systematic, intensive study of the dynamics of the interviewer–respondent relationship ought to be more strongly encouraged. For example, attention should be given to the possibility that, under pressure to respond, a respondent might forget something that he would normally have remembered; that is, under pressure, he might "want to forget." There is also the possibility that, to identify all the people attached to certain households, it may be necessary to employ an enumerator to ask more questions than those presently asked in a census, and to ask them developmentally—that is, each question building on the preceding answer. Finally, some recent work suggests that there are specific patterns of interviewer–respondent interaction that offer a respondent psychic rewards for providing accurate answers to certain kinds of questions that typically meet resistance.[9] Such questions and issues have relevance both for the problem of within-household underenumeration and for future interpretations and analyses of attitudinal questions of the sort that the Census Bureau and other government agencies are finding it increasingly necessary to ask.

Registration Systems

Although a system of individual registration may not be desirable in the United States, it does seem advisable to explore further the possibility of making being counted in the census an individual responsibility. For enumerating most of the population, the census is now, in effect, dependent upon an anthropological technique wherein someone reports for an assumed social group that is defined in terms of its attachment to a residential address. The census by mail is a move in the opposite direction, toward self-enumeration, but much is still unknown about the nature of household reporting on the mailed questionnaire. Moreover, large-scale registration systems— Internal Revenue, Social Security, Medicare—are being developed in the United States and may provide useful demographic data for a significant portion of the population. Technological innovations, such as the 1970 Census Address Coding Guide, may also make such

[9] See Kent Marquis, "The Effects of Social Reinforcement on Health Reporting in the Household Interview," *Sociometry,* 33, June 1970, pp. 203–215.

registration systems more available for demographic purposes.

Hence, *the Census Bureau, in cooperation with other interested statistical agencies, should undertake a series of pilot studies to determine if information from registration systems can be used to improve census coverage and accuracy further.*[10] For instance, Social Security numbers are used by the Medicare system and are collected by the monthly Current Population Survey. Thus, it may be possible, by matching Medicare records against household data collected in the CPS, to ascertain what proportion of persons listed by Medicare should be counted as members of households in the CPS sample but are not. While such a study would not be immediately addressed to the problem of underenumeration in the census, it would add to present understanding of the uses of an extensive registration system for improving census coverage.

Because errors in the registration of births and deaths influence estimates of net census undercount, *appropriate steps should also be taken to evaluate more frequently the registration of vital events and statistics on the number of individuals moving in and out of the country.* Knowledge that there are persons who are not enumerated by the census depends chiefly on information about annual numbers of births and deaths, since data indicating the number of people born each year are used in conjunction with data about mortality, immigration, and emigration, to ascertain how many people *should* be counted by a census. Yet, there has apparently never been a national investigation of the completeness of death registration. Nor was there a test of the completeness of birth registration between 1950 and 1970. A test of birth registration completeness has now been made in conjunction with the 1970 Census, and, since the study may shed some light on how many and which people were not counted in 1970, it should be supplemented by other, more frequent, investigations of the registration of vital events.

Record-Matching Experiments

On the assumption that everyone leaves some traces somewhere, sometime, census underenumeration (and census taking more generally) could be conceived as a problem of information retrieval. For

---

[10] A Census–Medicare match is already part of the 1970 Census Research and Evaluation Program. It will be used to evaluate *national* coverage of the population over 65. A preliminary 1960 Census–Medicare match suggests that the national estimates of undercoverage of the population in 1960 are high by about 250,000.

example, automated data processing techniques might be used to compare decennial census information on individual households with information on those same households obtained from other government or private record systems. If the number of individuals listed as resident at a given address were then found, by a computerized record-matching experiment, to exceed the number of individuals counted at that address in a recent census, the inconsistency would suggest "within-household" underenumeration.

The Census Bureau has undertaken numerous record-matching studies, including studies in connection with each of the last three decennial censuses. In 1950 and 1960, the technique was used both for estimating the accuracy of national census totals and for assessing the validity and reliability of recorded responses to the 25 percent census sample queries.[11] In 1970, it was used for content evaluation only, because, for reasons that are poorly understood,[12] previous record-matching studies had failed to achieve a sufficient number of matches to make fine coverage estimates possible.

---

[11] A description of the several studies will be found in U.S. Bureau of the Census, *Evaluation and Research Program of the U.S. Censuses of Population and Housing, 1960: Record Check Studies of Population Coverage,* Series ER 60, No. 2 (Washington, D.C.: U.S. Government Printing Office), 1964; and U.S. Bureau of the Census, *Evaluation and Research Program of the U.S. Censuses of Population and Housing, 1960: Accuracy of Data on Population Characteristics as Measured by CPS-Census Match,* Series ER 60, No. 5 (Washington, D.C.: U.S. Government Printing Office), 1964.

[12] For example, in 1960, record check studies were conducted on samples of four population groups: persons enumerated in the 1950 Census; children born during the intercensal period; persons missed in the 1950 Census but detected by the 1950 PES; aliens who registered with the Immigration and Naturalization Service in January 1960. Their combined representation is estimated to be 98 percent or more of the entire population.

Definite information about enumeration status was available for 6,003 sample persons; of these, 1.3 percent were identified as having been missed in the 1960 Census. Major limitations in the ability to arrive at precise estimates of omission arise from a failure to account for 16.5 percent of the working sample because of noninterviews, mostly caused by inability to obtain 1960 addresses for 932 sample persons and because of a probably missed group for whom a precise determination about inclusion in the 1960 Census could not be made.

Because noninterview and probably missed cases were believed to involve more underenumeration than the 6,003 cases for whom definite enumeration information was obtained, it did not appear reasonable to apply to the problem group the 1.3 percent missed rate established for the 6,003 persons of known enumeration status. Hence, various assumptions were made leading to a range of estimates of underenumeration. U.S. Bureau of the Census, ER 60, No. 2 *op. cit.,* pp. 1–2.

Written reports of the Census Bureau's record-matching experience, as well as discussions of known problems with individuals in and out of government who are involved in the development of computerized record systems, indicate three paramount difficulties. First, microfilmed census records (the only records that contain a counted person's name) are organized for permanent storage by geographic area. Thus, unless the place at which an individual was enumerated in a census is known, costly man-hours can be wasted looking for his form. (Moreover, if the individual were counted by "close-out" procedures, his name might not even appear on the microfilmed census schedule.) Second, it is only with the advent of the geographic coding system developed for the 1970 Census that *computerized* matching studies have begun to appear practical and sufficiently inexpensive. Third, until exploratory research of the sort recommended at other points in this report permits identification of the social characteristics associated with missed persons, it will be very difficult to know which record systems to match, assuming that missed persons are recorded somewhere. The Census Bureau has been inclined to regard current records, such as those maintained by employers and schools, as more useful than historical records, such as birth certificates,[13] because it is likely that not being counted in a census is symptomatic of not being identifiable in other nationally maintained record systems. But there has been no comprehensive exploration of the potential uses of current sources for improving coverage, as distinct from evaluating coverage and content.

A series of small-scale exploratory comparisons between local record sources and census records should be made. As a first step, census data should be compared with information derived from such sources as landlord and building superintendent directories, files on school dropouts, voter registration lists, unemployment benefit receipts, and driver licensing records. Later, the range should be broadened to include some of the less conventional record systems in which people make themselves visible or are made visible by others, such as the files of community legal clinics, storefront organizations, and health centers.

The objective of the research, at least at first, should not be to add people to totals derived from any particular census or survey, but rather to identify those record sources in which otherwise uncounted

---

[13] Morris Hansen, Leon Pritzker, and Joseph Steinberg, "The Evaluation and Research Program of the 1960 Census," *Proceedings of the Social Statistics Section of the American Statistical Association,* December 1959, p. 178.

people can be found. For example, clients of social service organizations could be interviewed, as people have been interviewed in "casual settings," and their enumeration status verified by comparison with census records. The technical obstacles to such arrangements remain large, but it seems theoretically possible to develop methods for matching the names of groups of geographically located individuals with census records to see which kinds of people may be missed by the census but recorded in other independent record systems.

Casual Interview Studies

As indicated in Chapter 2 (pp. 29–31), the Census Bureau, in cooperation with the Bureau of Labor Statistics, experimented with a "casual setting interview" procedure during the New Haven pretest and the Trenton dress rehearsal of the 1970 Census. Census enumerators interviewed men in bars, poolrooms, parks, restaurants, and on street corners. Data so obtained were then compared to census enumeration schedules to determine whether the interviewed persons had been counted at the places where they claimed to be living at the time of the interview.

The results were inconclusive. In Trenton, about 900 men were interviewed. Subsequent checking found that about one third could be identified as having been previously counted, that apparently one third had not been, and that the enumeration status of the remaining one third was impossible to determine.[14] Yet, since the procedure apparently does locate some men who are missed by conventional enumeration procedures, *additional casual interview studies should be conducted in connection with special censuses, or census pretests, in areas that presented acute enumeration problems in 1970.* Also, the Bureau should issue a technical paper summarizing the findings of the additional studies and comparing them with the results obtained in New Haven and Trenton.

Ethnographic Research

The Census Bureau specifically asked the Advisory Committee to assess the desirability of broadening the goals of its research program so as to help satisfy, through ethnographic research, the need of

[14] Deborah P. Klein, "Determining the Labor Force Status of Men Missed in the Census," U.S. Bureau of Labor Statistics, *Special Labor Force Report 114* (Washington, D.C.: U.S. Government Printing Office), March 1970, p. 30.

many government agencies for a better understanding of how people live in urban ghettos and other possibly "hard-to-enumerate" areas. At the time, the Bureau was already providing partial support for one ethnographic study being conducted in New York City. To perform the assessment task, the Advisory Committee established a Subcommittee on Urban Ethnography, which was charged with (a) considering the likelihood that replicating the New York study would lead to a better understanding of the factors associated with underenumeration and (b) depending upon the Subcommittee findings in that regard, stipulating the conditions under which replications would be most feasible and useful.[15] Although the Subcommittee conclusions were tentative (the New York study was then still in its preliminary stages), it did seem that, as a research technique, ethnographic research would prove a useful approach to gaining a better understanding of the causes of census underenumeration and that it certainly could provide the Bureau and others with insights into the social implications of various kinds of life circumstances.

Ethnographic, or participant–observer, studies of persons in extreme poverty, of ethnic or racial minorities, and of unusual population subgroups, such as practitioners of retreatist life styles (drug addicts, derelicts, wanderers) or experimenters in cooperative group living, may suggest ways of approaching the conceptual and instrumental issues raised by census undercounting. They can provide information leading to testable hypotheses about the meanings associated with concepts like "residence," "household," "time," and "kinship." They would increase existing knowledge about the social contexts into which the census-taking process intrudes and might also help to locate points at which difficult-to-enumerate groups would be suspicious, or accepting, of various data-collection instruments and procedures. Moreover, long-term ethnographic studies could generate local data bases that would serve a variety of comparative purposes, including record-matching experiments of the sort that the Census Bureau has done extensively, while simultaneously providing a first-hand look at the dynamics of enumeration-related social relationships and social processes.

In sum, *the Census Bureau would be well advised to join with other interested federal agencies in developing a planned participant–observer research program designed to improve understanding of*

---

[15] Further details will be found in National Research Council, Advisory Committee on Problems of Census Enumeration, *Interim Report,* November 1969, pp. 38–41. (Unpublished.)

government social data needs, the impediments to collecting neces-
sary information, and the difficulties involved in interpreting infor-
mation that has been or could be collected. Since organizing such a
coordinated effort can be complex and expensive, the initial steps
should be relatively modest and conservative, but they should be
taken with a view to building a solid participant–observer research
program that will eventually permit continuous analysis of styles of
life and significant social changes occurring at the family, neighborhood, and community levels.

The Bureau might begin, for example, by sharing selectively in the
support of participant–observer research projects sponsored by other
government agencies. However, the Bureau should also take preliminary steps to develop a quasi-intramural participant–observer program that can be made directly responsive to its own statutory responsibilities.

The Bureau has proposed, though it has not yet implemented, a
series of experiments with different types of participant–observers,
including Census Bureau employees and long-term community residents.[16] That proposal is a good one and deserves support, but it does
pose the risk that by using local residents as observers the Bureau may
be rendered vulnerable to some incident—a violation of confidentiality, perhaps—that could do considerable damage to other data-
collection programs. To avoid that danger, and also to enhance the
likelihood of success by developing a trusting, working relationship
with the community or neighborhood selected for study, it would,
therefore, seem wise for the Bureau to implement its proposal for the
use of resident–observers through arrangements with one or more
community organizations that would assist in selecting observers and
in supervising their activities.

Finally, the Bureau should undertake a systematic survey of participant–observer studies, planned or in progress, by university fac-

---

[16] As outlined, the project would be mainly "directed toward obtaining information on the nature of undercoverage in difficult-to-enumerate (essentially
ghetto) areas . . . concentrating on the kinds of persons who fail to be enumerated
. . . and the reasons why they are missed. . . . The proposal assumes that a resident of a specific area is in a good position to know about the number of living
quarters and persons in the area and that the resident's knowledge and acceptance in the community can be utilized in evaluating census coverage." U.S.
Bureau of the Census, "Analysis by Selected Ghetto Residents of Coverage in
Areas with Which They Are Intimately Acquainted," *Proposed Evaluation and
Research Program for the 1970 Censuses of Population and Housing,* Census
Bureau Memorandum, January 1969, p. 4. (Unpublished.)

ulty and senior graduate students, and then ask selected institutes and faculty so identified to nominate doctoral candidates, who, in return for partial Bureau support, would incorporate census-related research problems into their dissertation projects.

Using these several different approaches, the Bureau will be in a good position to obtain the direct, firsthand information that participant–observation can provide and that does not seem otherwise available. The Bureau should be cautioned, however, against the danger that too much might be expected from such studies within too short a period of time. The research products are likely to be hypotheses and rough sketches of behavioral, perceptual, and value patterns typically couched in tentative, exploratory terms. They may not provide definitive answers to census counting problems, but they may make it easier to decide what kinds of questions need to be asked about the census and how best to ask them.

Longitudinal Studies

In order to learn more about anonymity as a stage in a career, and about the social settings in which persons with strong preferences for anonymity are likely to become visible, *an intensive survey should be made of the difficulties encountered in conducting longitudinal studies by social scientists, the Census Bureau itself, and others. In addition, thorough analysis should be made of the characteristics of dropouts from longitudinal studies, and modest longitudinal studies of groups drawn from populations that might be expected to prefer social invisibility should be initiated.*

An investigation should be made of the difficulties encountered in long-term studies of special subpopulations, such as psychiatric patients, college graduates, gifted children, engaged couples, and participants in fertility and family planning surveys. Since the difficulties experienced in longitudinal studies are usually noted only in passing in the published research findings, a survey of the experiences of principal investigators, by questionnaire or interview, may yield fruitful information about the social characteristics of the subjects who are most difficult to locate, the procedures employed in attempts to locate them, and the conditions found to be associated with the failure or success of such efforts. Such a study would be an appropriate subject for dissertation research.[17]

[17] The National Center for Educational Statistics in the U.S. Office of Education (HEW) is currently supporting research by the Center for the Study of Eval-

A closely related research project would be detailed analysis of the characteristics of dropouts from panel studies. Consider the following example: An attempt is made to interview a sample of persons at the same address twice in two years. Some are found in the first year, but not in the second. If the characteristics of those found both times are compared with the characteristics of persons missing the second time, insights might be gained into the factors associated with the latter group becoming lost. Such an approach would have two advantages: It would require no new data,[18] and it would help to isolate and identify some of the very small groups that are thought to compose the underenumerated population.

One or more longitudinal studies should also be undertaken of samples drawn from populations that, for various reasons, might be expected to prefer social invisibility—for example, paroled convicts, former mental patients, rehabilitated drug users, or persons in arrears on alimony or child-support payments. Since the addresses of such individuals are frequently known because of legal requirements or organizational record-keeping practices, it should be possible to check periodically to see whether or not the individuals in question actually reside at their recorded addresses.

Such periodic checks could yield at least three kinds of useful information: broadly identified categories of persons who are likely to be missed in a census or other social survey; descriptions of the individual and social characteristics of such persons (as recorded by the agencies concerned with them); and clues to some of the conditions associated with such persons becoming "lost." Although the information gathered may not result directly in adding names to the census roster, an understanding of the processes by which individuals become invisible to various social-control agencies, and by which they maintain their invisibility, will suggest alternative means of counting or estimating the number of persons missed because they have some special reason for wanting to elude the census enumerator.

---

uation, Graduate School of Education, University of California at Los Angeles, in which a number of characteristics of existing longitudinal studies are being analyzed. Among the topics being studied are the problems of locating interviewed persons for follow-up sessions.

[18] The Census Bureau, for example, has extensive records on tape from the Current Population Survey.

6   Analytical Methods

Demographic methods that lead to national estimates of census underenumeration cannot now be used to develop undercount estimates for regions, states, metropolitan areas, and other relatively small geographic areas. A major reason is the lack of accurate information on population migration within the nation. As frequently noted in this volume and elsewhere, however, many census users have policy and program interests that are frustrated by the lack of reliable census counts or estimates for small areas.

This chapter describes—in outline form—several analytical methods that should be explored in the search for reasonably accurate small-area population statistics. Except for one experimental approach described at the end of the chapter, all the methods use existing data from census or other sources. The analytical methods are discussed in a simple, schematic way. No pretense is made of presenting fully detailed formulations or solutions. Specific illustrations are presented to make a point concrete rather than as definitive prescriptions.

The approaches discussed primarily reflect standard statistical ideas. Some may help to explore hypotheses about the nature and causes of underenumeration. Others might lead to specific methods of adjusting small-area population counts for underenumeration. The principal recommendation of the chapter is that *increased support should be given to analytical studies of small-area underenumeration (as well as of other sources of census error) with the objectives of discovering which demographic, economic, and other characteristics of an area are associated with enumeration error and devising methods for adjusting small-area census counts.*

The Need for Small-Area Population Statistics

The Census Bureau and other government agencies are well aware of the need for a method of apportioning the national estimate of underenumeration in the 1970 Census among regions, states, counties, cities, and other small areas. In general, however, the Bureau has hesitated to make adjustments in direct counts because of the large methodological problems involved and because of the damage that could be done by publication of seriously erroneous estimates. It is essential to remember that census counts are an important part of the political process. In any disputed counting situation, there are likely to be special interests with a stake in having the official counts altered in one direction or another. An adjustment procedure that is open to criticism on methodological grounds could thus stimulate larger controversies than those it was intended to allay. Also, because of the interlocking structure of the federal statistical system, adjustments in the counts for one set of localities, or for one set of distributions in an official statistical series, might necessitate corresponding changes for other localities and for many other statistical series. Such difficulties might, of course, be mitigated by simultaneous publication of both direct and estimated counts or by an understanding that different adjustments, or no adjustment, might be appropriate in different circumstances. Electoral districting, for example, might be strictly based on unadjusted counts for constitutional reasons, if for no other.

If it were possible, even at great expense, to obtain complete enumerations in some areas as part of a controlled field study, then standard statistical methodology could be brought to bear directly on the relationship between census underenumeration and social, demographic, and economic variables. In fact, however, it is possible to be secure in accepting an enumeration as almost error-free only in extraordinary cases, such as a count of the population of a prison. More is to be learned about what participant–observation can accomplish with regard to counts of small segments of the population. Nevertheless, any attack on the small-area estimation problem may necessarily be one in which the key dependent variable—the number of uncounted persons—is not observable.

There may be no reasonable alternative to using some theoretical construct, sometimes a quite modest one, in order to come to grips with the problem. For example, it would not be unreasonable to assume that frequent nonresponse to key census questions (or nonresponse because no one is found at home and census data are therefore obtained by a close-out procedure) is associated with underenumeration. If it can then be understood how frequency of such cases, which is measurable, is connected with income level, educational level, and so on, progress will have been made in understanding underenumeration. At the very least, informed guidance will be gained about where to concentrate enumeration efforts.

Indirect measurement—the use of proxy variables—is common in science. To measure the distance from the earth to the sun, no one climbs out into space with surveyors' tape or yardsticks. Rather, indirect measurements are used, together with a theory that is trusted. In the underenumeration case, however, the use of proxy variables is less attractive for at least two reasons. First, there are no accepted models or theories for connecting undercounting with indirect measurements. Second, there appears to be a tendency to regard population counting as amenable to substantial improvement. What can be accomplished on the second point remains unknown, although in some other cultures the problem of undercounting seems to be less serious. The first point, however, suggests the utility of examining patterns of census response—an activity that might be much facilitated by groundwork of the kind described in this chapter.

Demographic Accounting

A commonly used approach to enumeration problems might be called "demographic accounting." A simplified example will illustrate. To arrive at the United States population as of the end of 1965, compute:

1960 population (census), *plus*
births from April 1, 1960 through the end of 1965 (birth registration), *minus*
deaths from April 1, 1960 to the end of 1965 (death registration), *plus*
immigration *less* emigration from April 1, 1960 through the end of 1965 (immigration data and other sources).

In the above form of accounting, oversimplified for expository purposes, all the data are taken as precisely what they are represented to be,[1] although in actual use there must be adjustments for estimated

[1] See Ansley J. Coale, "The Population of the United States in 1950 Classified by Age, Sex, and Color—A Revision of Census Figures," *Journal of the*

errors in the individual components.[2] The major appeal of the method is its direct nature. Its use by Coale and others and by the Census Bureau has served to provide fundamental measurements of national underenumeration.

The accounting method, however, has limitations. It does not use relevant independent variables, such as collected sales taxes or amount of water consumed. The selection of procedures for adjusting counts is partly arbitrary, and the arithmetic procedures do not lend themselves to simple measurements of uncertainty. It is only fair to add, of course, that these problems occur with other approaches as well.

The most important limitation of demographic accounting, however, is that reasonably adequate migration data are available only for the nation as a whole. This is lamentable not only because of its consequences for demographic accounting, but also because internal migration data of good quality would have other scientific, business, and administrative values. The relative costs of improved census coverage and improved migration data are not clear, but it should be noted that improved migration data obtained annually, even without improved coverage, would yield better underenumeration estimates and, hence, population estimates.

In contrast to demographic accounting, the analytic methods presented here are applicable to small areas, but the interpretation of their conclusions will be more ambiguous.

The discussion that follows is divided into four parts. In the first, plausible but admittedly crude assumptions are used to construct *simple demographic models*. For example, assume that at working ages the white and nonwhite sex ratios are the same in an area. Also assume that whites of both sexes and nonwhite females are counted

---

American Statistical Association, 50, 1955, pp. 15–64; Ansley J. Coale and Melvin Zelnik, *New Estimates of Fertility and Population in the United States: A Study of Annual White Births from 1855 to 1960 and of Completeness of Enumeration in the Censuses from 1880 to 1960* (Princeton, New Jersey: Princeton University Press), 1963; and U.S. Bureau of the Census, *Current Population Reports*, Series P-25, No. 310, "Estimates of the Population of the United States and Components of Change, by Age, Color, and Sex: 1950 to 1960," June 30, 1965.

[2] See U.S. Bureau of the Census, *Current Population Reports*, Series P-25, No. 442, "Estimates of the Population of the United States and Components of Change, 1940–1970," March 20, 1970; and Donald S. Akers, "Immigration Data and National Population Estimates for the United States," *Demography*, 4, 1967, pp. 262–272.

accurately enough. Then, without using counts of nonwhite males, simple ratio estimates of that population segment can be prepared. Enumeration problem areas would be suggested by large discrepancies between estimates and counts.

In the second section, an *outlier analysis* of the following form is proposed: Working with specified areas—for example, counties—consider as possible dependent variables various functions of a three-way cross-classification containing counts by age, race, and sex. As independent variables, use available area data, such as measures of industrialization and proportion of high school graduates. It is hoped that much of the variation in the dependent variables will be explained by the variation in the independent variables. Presuming that this is the case, for those relatively few counties in which the observed and predicted values are widely separated, the demographer would be alerted to unexplained variation that might well be symptomatic of an enumeration error.

The third method is concerned with variables that appear to be related to the number of undercounted individuals in an area. These *proxy variables*, called response failure (RF) variables, are treated as dependent in a regression analysis. Explained variation in the dependent variables may be symptomatic of enumeration problems, and outliers might point to important independent variables that need later introduction.

Finally, several *experimental procedures* for evaluating the effectiveness of enumeration protocols[3] are discussed. A protocol that can be administered in two phases results in the measurement of *gain*. Also considered are experiments involving comparison of several protocols through the use of designed randomized experiments.

In summary, a variety of approaches is suggested to give insight into the sources of enumeration problems. Some may develop into useful techniques for estimating underenumeration in small areas. In working on these problems, one should keep in mind that a good solution contains within itself estimates of its own errors.

Simple Demographic Models

It is possible that an appreciation of the orders of magnitude of census undercounting in small areas would be obtained by exploring easily applied and conceptually simple demographic techniques. For

---

[3]For purposes of present exposition, a census protocol is the entire process by which a census is taken. In particular, a two-wave census procedure might be

example, a simple method for adjusting small-area census counts is based on the assumption that age-specific sex ratios (number of males to number of females) are the same for nonwhites and whites. The procedure would be the following:

1. Only male nonwhite counts are to be adjusted.
2. For age group g in geographic area a compute for the white strata the sex ratio $= \dfrac{\text{number of males}}{\text{number of females}} = r_{ag}$.
3. Multiply the counted number of nonwhite females in area a and age group g by r_{ag}. The product is the adjusted count for nonwhite males.

Such a procedure is unusual in that nonwhite male counts are never used. A basic premise is that nonwhite female and white counts are more accurate than nonwhite male counts. (The various studies using demographic accounting suggest that this is true at the national level.) It is a simple procedure to apply. The decennial census supplies the three required counts, and the procedure might be used even when the area in (3) is a subarea of the area in (2). The results may point to likely sources of enumeration problems when the computed and observed area populations differ widely. The usefulness of the method can be examined by repeated comparisons of estimated counts for a large area with the appropriate sums of estimated counts for their smaller subareas. The plausibility of the assumptions in the model can be examined with national census data.

Many variations of such simple demographic models could also be explored. A minor variation, for instance, would be to treat the nonwhite male counts as correct for the youngest and oldest age brackets, adjusting only the intervening age categories. A more complicated example might be based on a premise such as: The nonwhite sex ratio for ages 9–12 is the same as the nonwhite sex ratio for ages 20–24, with the age 9–12 sex ratio being obtained directly from census counts. By looking at several such models and comparing their accumulated results with the results of a census and of studies of national undercounts using demographic methods, large discrepancies are likely to be found, which may indicate the existence of enumeration problems.

---

regarded as providing two protocols: The first providing counts from the first wave, and the second providing counts from both waves together.

Sex–Race–Age Cross-Classification Analysis

The occurrence of unusual sex ratios may be evidence of census undercounting. Such evidence emerges in the following form: Cross-
classify the population of an area by age (perhaps five classes), sex
(two classes), and race (white and nonwhite). For each age class,
compare the white and nonwhite sex ratios. In some areas, the ratios
for working-age nonwhites will be consistently less than the corresponding ratios for whites, and when that occurs, the findings may
be taken as evidence of undercounting, although it is possible that
the low sex ratios occur for other reasons. For example, it is well
known that there is an unusually large proportion of females in the
District of Columbia and an unusually large proportion of males in
Alaska. The sex ratios in both cases are presumably attributable to
features of the local occupational structure.

There is one strategy for making this kind of inquiry more exact,
one that to the knowledge of the Committee has never been carried
out. It involves, first, a statistical analysis of three-way age–race–sex
tables for a variety of areas to obtain some idea of the inherent dispersion and the most useful mathematical functions (for example,
weighted averages, or weighted averages of logarithms) of the cell
relative frequencies. Then, area-specific pieces of information of the
sort suggested by the District of Columbia and Alaska examples are
added and a regression analysis carried out. From this, it may be possible to identify a small class of areas giving rise to outliers (that is,
areas whose cell-frequency functions are remarkably poorly explained by the best explanation for the areas as a group). Such outliers may indicate undercounting.

Specifically, the Committee's proposal is to prepare from the 1960
and 1970 Censuses three-way tables by age by sex by race, one table
for each selected area under study. Two racial groups would be used,
and age would be classified into a small number of categories. A
choice of kind of area would also be required, and, for each area
studied, a variety of other pieces of possibly relevant information
would have to be specified—for example, physical area, mean temper-
ature, industrial structure, proportion of adult population married,
and something relating to socioeconomic level.

The problem then becomes one of data analysis—to find simple
and relevant functions of the three-way cross-classification frequencies (say, ratios of frequencies, linear combinations of logarithms of
frequencies) that are well explained by simple functions, preferably

linear, of the other pieces of information. Any such explanatory relationship will give an estimated regression, together with scatter around the regression. If some areas correspond to large outliers from an estimated regression, they should then be examined more closely to see if they have characteristics that may reasonably give rise to underenumeration.

Consider an oversimplified hypothetical example in which the sex ratios of a number of geographic units, without reference to race, for people at ages 18–35, are compared with a measure of industrialization. If the units are counties, the data might look something like the dots in Figure 1. A line, shown in the figure, could be estimated to fit the cloud of dots fairly well, thereby providing both an estimated relationship and an estimated scatter around it.

If, then, one of the counties examined has a sex ratio and industrial structure that give rise to the cross in the figure, well away from the cloud of dots for other counties, the county is an outlier with respect to the linear relationship, and a fair inference might be made that the outlying county is one with serious underenumeration. If such an inference is made, moreover, an improved estimate of the county's sex ratio becomes feasible from the estimated linear relationship, and from that some inference about underenumeration is possible.

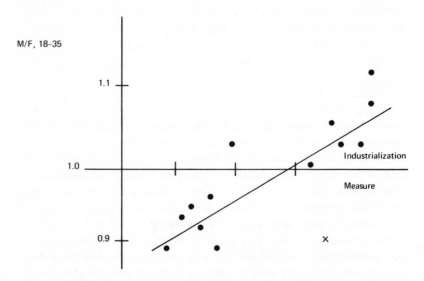

FIGURE 1   Simple example of suggested approach—hypothetical data.

The success of the research would, of course, depend to a large extent on the skill and industry of the individuals who carry it out. It requires competent demographic, economic, and sociological background work to find appropriate independent variables as well as statistical ability to carry out the analysis.

The research will never prove that one factor or another is the cause of underenumeration. Even if outliers are found, they may stem from other sources of error, such as systematic misclassifications. But the analysis may make plausible some causes of underenumeration and may be useful when placed together with wholly different lines of attack, such as skilled participant–observation.

At a minimum, research of this kind should be juxtaposed with the other approaches described in this chapter. Certainly, the resulting estimated regression equations will be worth study for the light they shed on the relationship between exogenous variables and age, sex, and race combinations. Ideally, however, the research will improve present understanding of the socioeconomic factors closely associated with census undercounting.

One final qualification: The proposal rests squarely on the presumption that there are relatively few areas that are highly prone to underenumeration—that is, that most areas are subject to about the same rate of undercounting. If, on the contrary, there is a more or less continuous spectrum of rates of underenumeration, the proposed research is less likely to yield the desired results, but the research may still be of interest in other respects.

Proxies for the Missing Dependent Variable (the Number Not Enumerated)

To apply regression techniques, it is necessary to have values, or at least estimated values, of the dependent variable. In the case of census undercounts, the only currently accepted estimates—actual number less counted number in a stratum—are at the national level, and even they are not firm estimates. Hence, regression techniques are usable for studying underenumeration in smaller areas only indirectly by finding proxies for the missing dependent variable.

It is hardly surprising that proxies are hard to find and that, if some are chosen, their utility is difficult to assess. It is desirable that proxy variables be easy to measure and have a substantial portion of their variation explained by available socioeconomic independent variables. The most important aspect of the proxy variables, however, is that they should be closely related to the dependent variable. Under fortunate circumstances, the estimated regression of a proxy variable on the socioeconomic independent variables may be more closely associated with undercounts than the proxy variable itself. This could happen if, for example, the proxy variable has a high chance variability, but the estimated expectation of the proxy variable a relatively low variability.

There should be serious exploration of the degree to which uncounted persons share characteristics of persons who give incomplete or inaccurate responses to the census—that is, of the frequency of incomplete or inaccurate responses as a useful proxy for the undercount. Although there is now no reason to assert that underenumeration is related to an association between the demographic characteristics of the underenumerated and census field-office difficulties, the possibility should be investigated further. At a minimum, research in this area should identify areas in which census field difficulties are likely to be encountered.

A small subgroup of the Advisory Committee, the Subcommittee on Data Analysis, performed a series of exploratory analyses to determine the relationship between certain specifiable characteristics of cities—for example, the nonwhite proportion of the population in 1960, the proportion employed in manufacturing, the number of single-unit housing structures—and measures of nonresponse, such as percent of population imputed for omissions due to noninterview.[4] An important independent variable was found to be the change in the nonwhite percentage of the population of an area between 1950 and 1960. The units used were some 600 cities. The simple correlation between the independent variable, percent change in the nonwhite population, and the dependent variable, percent substitutions for nonresponse in the census, was .362, and somewhat larger with other proxy variables. Using several independent variables, a multiple correlation coefficient of about 0.6 was obtained for prediction of percent substitution. Thus, about 36 percent of the variance in percent substitution was linearly accounted for.

Since the use of proxy variables regressed on area-characteristic variables appears to be a useful source of information about enumeration difficulties, and since the information gained could be immediately useful in developing strategies for the allocation of census-taking resources, such analyses should be continued. Although at this

---

[4] A more detailed description of the project will be found in Appendix B.

point it does not seem that quantitative estimates of undercount can be obtained from the use of proxy variables, further research may lead to a more optimistic view. For example, the use of Social Security and other independent records may permit very accurate counts by areas for special groups—counts that could then be compared with the proxy variables to examine directly the degree of association.

In addition to the interest held by the nature and magnitude of explanation of a proxy variable by independent socioeconomic variables, there may also be utility in examining areas giving rise to large residuals—areas for which the difference between the proxy and its regression estimate is unusually large. Such cases may draw attention to neglected independent variables and other deficiencies in the model.

In that respect, the approach of this section resembles the outlier analysis proposed earlier. There are two major differences: In the outlier analysis, the dependent variables would arise in part from the analysis itself and not only from general socioeconomic insight, as in the proxy variable approach; and the dependent variables in the outlier analysis need have no obvious relationship to underenumeration. By the same token, the regression relationships (in the outlier analysis) are not likely to be of interest *per se*, but only insofar as they lead to interesting outliers (that is, large residuals).

Experiments with Census Protocols

One standard approach to an operational definition of census undercounting is to compare the observed counts obtained by two or more enumeration procedures. That is, if two census protocols[5] are used to perform a census on the same population, the observed difference in the resulting counts could be taken as a measure of the extent of underenumeration associated with each. Such an experiment would not indicate the difference between true and observed counts, but it would provide the difference in the two counts achieved and thus, presumably, indicate the differential effectiveness of the two protocols employed. (It would, of course, be well also to look at other measures of comparative effectiveness, such as a relative difference, e.g., a difference divided by the average of the two counts.)

Further, one census protocol could include another; this might be called "nesting." In the 1970 Census, the self-enumeration and

<hr />

[5] See note 3, p. 103.

follow-up interview procedures were supplemented in many areas by mover checks and "Were You Counted?" campaigns. The number of persons added by such additional efforts was tallied separately, providing, in effect, a direct measure of the difference in undercounting between the more restrictive protocol, if used alone, and the more extensive protocol actually used. In other words, assuming careful record keeping, a portion of the actual 1970 Census operation can be regarded as an experiment of the sort proposed.[6]

One of the great advantages of such experiments is, in fact, their adaptability to regular census operations—that is, the possibility of conducting them under actual "census conditions." But perhaps their greatest advantage is that they provide an opportunity for further analysis of both the ecological variables associated with large counting differences and the demographic and social characteristics of persons added to census totals by intensive enumeration procedures. It would be possible, for example, to regress observed differences in the results obtained by different "nested" protocols against socioeconomic variables for the experimental areas. Information would thereby be obtained both about how those variables are associated with large counting differences and about the appropriateness of different protocols for different kinds of areas.

Similarly, the proposed experiments would make it possible to identify more directly and to measure the social and behavioral characteristics of the unenumerated population—that is, those added in the second wave of a two-wave protocol pair. Such characteristics, which are purported to describe (and predict) the response of localized groups to changing social and economic circumstances, are, as indicated at many points in this report, of prime concern to those who formulate and administer public policies based on information derived from census statistics. Simply being able to determine that the characteristics of added persons do not differ markedly from those of the counted population would be an important gain, allowing always for the possibility that the observed units of this "missed" (i.e., previously missed but subsequently found) population will forever remain unrepresentative of the "never found" popula-

[6]The Bureau has conducted a number of experiments along these lines. See, for example, U.S. Bureau of the Census, "The 1950 Censuses—How They Were Taken," in *Procedural Studies of the 1950 Censuses*, No. 2 (Washington, D.C.: U.S. Government Printing Office), 1955, p. 6, for information on the work that was done in Cape Girardeau and Perry County, Missouri, in the spring of 1948.

tion. First, however, it is necessary to locate *and* identify the individuals to be studied, and the advantage of the proposed experiments is that they will, if successful, do both, thus making it possible to describe directly the social and behavioral characteristics of at least some undercounted persons.

In addition to nested protocols, there may be useful experiments on two or more protocols that intrinsically cannot be nested—for example, two quite different methods of training or supervising enumerators. In such cases, a single area cannot receive both protocols. The simplest experimental design would select at random areas for each of the two protocols. It would doubtless be more efficient to form pairs of similar areas and then assign at random one treatment to each member of a pair. The same approach, using homogeneous collections of areas, might be used if there are more than two distinct protocols.

These experiments would be costly, but they could be very informative when carefully designed. Thus, when considering such protocol comparisons, every effort should be made to think in terms of designed and controlled experiments, including appropriate randomization, as has frequently been done in experiments conducted by the Census Bureau in the past.

The intent of the constitutional provision that calls for a determination once every decade of how many people there are and where
they are was broadened even at the time of the first population census in 1790, and it has been further amplified as the nation has
evolved into a large, complex society. Effective government requires
more information about the population than simply how big it is,
where it is concentrated, and how it is composed by age, sex, and
race. Knowledge is needed about how the several parts of the society
do or do not fit together, about the varied forms of social organization that exist, and about how much and in which directions those
forms are changing.

An immediate concern of this report has been the possibility that
some people are not counted in censuses because the social circumstances and behaviors that distinguish them as "persons" are not adequately comprehended by census counting instruments and categories
of social identification. More generally, however, the Committee has
hoped to draw attention to the implications for research of treating
census underenumeration not simply as a residual product of established enumeration procedures, but also as an indication that the society is organized in ways that are more complex than the enumeration
procedures and classificatory frameworks of censuses and social surveys usually suggest.

If, for example, it were discovered that a chief cause of underenumeration is the assumption in the census that most people have clear,
easily definable attachments to a specific address—or conversely,
that the lack of such attachments is neither peculiarly nor persis-
tently characteristic of any particular social stratum—might it not

seem worthwhile to explore further the advantages of taking the entire census on a *de facto*[1] basis? If it were found that the number and characteristics of uncounted persons could be estimated from information contained in other record systems, might it seem sensible to ask how such systems could be better used to supplement or augment information collected from persons regularly counted in the decennial censuses?

These are difficult issues. The fact that they are raised here should not be construed as an indication of agreement with critics of the census who contend that there is unwarranted redundancy in the federal statistical system, that the number of questions asked in the census ought to be reduced, or that the federal government should move in the direction of establishing a national data bank of sufficient scope and depth to make the decennial censuses unnecessary. Rather, what ought to be emphasized is that the identification of underenumeration as a troublesome statistical deficiency both underscores the need and provides the opportunity to examine carefully the full range of data-gathering instruments and classificatory arrangements that might be used to improve the products of the federal social data-gathering enterprise.[2]

Alternative Census and Survey Methods

There are very practical reasons why the broad research implications of census underenumeration are worth stressing. In the first place, there has not been sufficient exploration of alternative methods of conducting censuses and social surveys. The Census of Population was originally conducted household by household, because, at the time, the family residence was one of a very small number of continuously functioning centers of social communication. Today, however, the Censuses of Population and Housing serve many disparate objectives, which, at least on the surface, do not all seem to require that every counted person be attached to an enumerated residence. For instance, although it is constitutionally required that all individuals in every political subdivision be counted for representation purposes, there is no constitutional stipulation that data on the social

---

[1] That is, counting people where they are found, rather than where they live. See note 2, p. 59.

[2] Comments along these same lines have occasionally been voiced by others. See, for example, Harry M. Rosenberg, "Census Data and the Analysis of Social Trends," *The American Statistician*, December 1971, pp. 24–27.

characteristics of the population be collected for those same areas. Hence, it seems reasonable to ask why further efforts should not be made to develop alternative record systems in such a way that at least some of the characteristics of small-area populations could be estimated by making use of such information as the number and kinds of dependents claimed by local taxpayers, the number of registered automobiles, licensed drivers, Social Security beneficiaries, children attending school, and the like.

Second, the question of timeliness has a significant bearing on the relationship between improving census coverage and a more general improvement in the quality of census data. If 1970 Census data, particularly small-area data, are used to make formula-grant allocations in 1979, it can be anticipated that the distortions introduced by the age of the statistics will be greater, despite various adjustments, than any reasonable estimate of counting error at the time the data were collected. A quinquennial census may be an urgent need. More frequent special-purpose or supplemental censuses and surveys may also be required. Yet, to speak of a marked increase in the number and variety of social data collection efforts is to raise the specter of greater costs and, thus, to suggest again the utility of exploring alternative methods of collecting needed supplementary information.

Third, if it is true that the geographic mobility of the population is increasing, that people are developing more varied life styles, and that they are becoming more protective not so much of their anonymity as of their privacy, conventional censuses and social surveys may become increasingly difficult to conduct. One obvious weakness of the 1970 Census, as well as of earlier censuses, was the relatively lengthy period that elapsed in some areas between the initial mailing of the census questionnaire in late March and final completion of the canvass. In Detroit, the Census Bureau was still attempting to hire enumerators late in May; in New York City, even later. Thus, follow-up work for the 1970 Census was going on in June, perhaps even in July, long after most school systems had closed for the year and at a time when, in any event, approximately four percent of the population can be expected to change its place of residence.

Finally, new technologies are emerging that promise to make certain kinds of social data collection easier and less costly than present census-taking procedures. The pace of developmental research on intercomputer communication, for example, makes it reasonable to expect that in the early 1980's a decentralized, but nonetheless coherent, national data center will have emerged without ever being officially established. Such a development will surely present new possibilities, as well as new problems, for those concerned with facilitating user access to census data, but it will probably also create new opportunities for improving census coverage, and for more frequent updating of census information, that would not be envisaged if reducing underenumeration were considered solely in terms of census canvasses.

The Question of Privacy

There are, of course, important legal and ethical issues involved in efforts to develop alternative or supplemental methods of improving the census. Some of the measures that might be used would require changes in the law. For example, many administrative record systems are legally accessible to the Census Bureau and a number have been used in matching studies. Others, however, have not been accessible. If matching certain other governmental records with census data were thought a useful way of locating missed persons, legal or administrative restrictions on the Census Bureau's inspection and use of those records might have to be removed.

Still other proposals, though they might not raise direct legal problems, would call into question the value the society places on privacy. If computer-stored information gathered by several different agencies (governmental and nongovernmental) were made accessible by data-bank centralization, or by the development of computer programs facilitating a search for data pertaining to the same individual in many different record systems, privacy might suffer because of the new vulnerability of the system to penetration by strangers. In other words, some efforts to improve census coverage might lead to encroachments and harassment for all citizens—not merely for the uncounted—although they might bear unequally on different sectors or classes.

It might be objected that the privacy costs of, for example, efforts to reduce underenumeration can be regarded as marginal to the privacy costs already being incurred by other decisions and events. But the Committee would prefer to turn the question around and suggest that, *prima facie,* the benefit to be obtained from such undertakings is not worth more than a very small additional privacy cost.

Effective safeguards against the mentioned types of encroachment or harassment could modify the reckoning of cost and benefit. The Committee has not examined possible technological safeguards thoroughly, nor has it carefully considered the several managerial solutions that have been advanced in various quarters.[3] In fact, the Committee applauds the careful concern for confidentiality that the Census Bureau has maintained and appreciates the conscientiousness with which the Bureau has sought to avoid breaches of individual privacy in giving users access to its aggregated data. It is only because such restrictions may not suffice in the future that the Committee thinks it necessary to call attention to the potential dangers and to urge that the development of new census and survey procedures be accompanied by efforts to provide adequate protective arrangements.

The Need for Cooperative Research Programs

These long-term prospects and issues suggest a need both for forward-looking statistical policies and for an extension of research activity in many areas. On the policy side, to recommend ways of using new technological developments more effectively, the Committee would have to have a better acquaintance with the intricacies of the federal statistical system than it has been able to acquire. With regard to matters affecting future research, however, it seems clear that the diversity of research activities and competence that would be required for a systematic attack on problems of census data collection and use points to a need for greater cooperation and coordination among the many potential sponsors of research on census and survey problems. Indeed, even at the federal level, it seems undesirable, as well as impractical, to expect one agency, or small group of agencies, to assume the full burden of organizing, funding, and supervising such efforts.

As indicated in Chapter 3 and elsewhere in this report, a central objective of a research program addressed to the problems involved in counting and describing people should be to encourage continuing and intimate collaboration between demographers, statisticians, and

---

[3] For example,

● To give any individual (free) access, at reasonably frequent intervals, not only to what he or his representative has at some time put into the government's data archives, but also to all the information about him reposing in those archives

● To enable anyone to supply information correcting or countering the data in his file

● To enable anyone to know, at reasonably frequent intervals, which agencies, offices, branches, have access to which items of the data in his file

survey methodologists, on one hand, and, on the other, social scientists, who, by training or research experience in other fields, may be able to shed additional light on census-taking difficulties. In the present context of federal agency support for research on social problems, this suggests that much stronger efforts should be made to join the kinds of social science competence found on the staffs and in the external research communities of some of the principal social data *users* with the kinds of scientific expertise that have been well developed by the principal data *producers*. Given the limited funding available for support of completely new areas of research, such an integrative approach may be necessary on practical grounds, but also it offers the advantage, in principal, of directly linking research on substantive policy issues to research on the information base used in policy design and implementation.

There are, however, important obstacles to successful organization of the broad range of research capabilities that might be brought to bear on social data collection and use problems. One, certainly, is the perceptions that many of the potential government research sponsors have of one another and of their appropriate roles within the federal statistical system. The Census Bureau has traditionally been viewed, and has tended to view itself, as providing a data collection service for operating agencies that have large statistical information requirements. Some agencies, such as the Bureau of Labor Statistics and the National Center for Health Statistics, actively participate in designing, analyzing, and publishing the results of government surveys adapted to their special needs, but much of the design work, and the actual collection of the data, is often carried out by the Census Bureau.

This functional division of labor has both advantages and costs. It permits a few important user agencies to take advantage of the methodological competence and physical facilities of the Census Bureau and, at the same time, to maintain considerable control over the scope and content of surveys that they contract with the Census Bureau to perform. It enables some users to press for or to undertake special kinds of experimentation and analysis in areas that appear to require further methodological or conceptual development. In some instances, however, this institutionalized separation of the data collection and data analysis functions may promote a division of methodological and substantive research interests that impedes efforts to address problems that embrace both.

Institutional separation is not a serious problem if work is approached jointly. When representatives of the Census Bureau and the Bureau of Labor Statistics discuss a change in the content of the Current Population Survey, their negotiations are facilitated by a shared understanding of the substantive information needs of the one and the data-gathering capabilities of the other. The two agencies have a long history of cooperative involvement in statistical program development, punctuated by frequent interchange of professional personnel.

In other cases, however, the Census Bureau, by virtue of its emphasis on methodological problems, appears to be regarded by other agencies as insufficiently sympathetic to their information needs. This seems to be the case particularly with some of the newer federal agencies and those without well-developed statistical programs of their own.

A second, related obstacle to encouraging broader sponsorship of research on census-taking problems is the present pattern of potentially co-optable research resources, which tends to be fragmented along agency and disciplinary lines. The Census Bureau invests much of its research and development budget[4] in work on survey methods and theory, questionnaire design, response errors, equipment design and utilization, computer editing, administrative control, and techniques of statistical analysis.[5] Similarly, the Bureau of Labor Statistics has recently allocated $100,000 to a program of "research and evaluation of statistical techniques, methodologies, and information processing systems" that will lead to improvements in the quality of national labor statistics.[6] However, the areas selected for research emphasis contrast sharply with those stressed by some of the major user agencies that support research on substantive issues that are nonetheless relevant to the improvement of census data quality.

Part of the Fiscal Year 1972 budget request of the Office of Economic Opportunity, for example, is for support of work on the social psychology of poverty. The budget of the Manpower Administration of the Department of Labor includes several external research programs addressed to the social, economic, and psychological dimen-

[4] The budget for research and development related to all Bureau activities, of which the Census of Population is only one.
[5] See *The Budget of the United States Government, Fiscal Year 1972– Appendix* (Washington, D.C.: U.S. Government Printing Office), 1971, p. 225.
[6] Executive Office of the President, Office of Management and Budget, "Principal Statistical Budgets and Programs for Fiscal Year 1971," *Statistical Reporter*, March 1971, p. 152.

sions of chronic unemployment, and the Department of Housing and Urban Development will use some of its funds to promote studies of urban–rural migration. Yet, because of the way in which these research concerns are presently defined—that is, because of the way in which their relationship to performance of each agency's mission is presently viewed—their relevance to work on improving the quality of the national social data base is often inadequately perceived.

A third impediment to developing a more broadly based program of enumeration research stems from the uneven research and research sponsorship experience of the many federal agencies that are or should be directly concerned with improving census data quality. Agencies like the Census Bureau and the Bureau of Labor Statistics have long been involved in data-collection research and analysis. The Census Bureau, in particular, might be regarded as a model government research institution worthy of emulation in many respects. It has a highly trained staff, close ties with a set of professional communities, and stringent standards and procedures for review and analysis of work that it undertakes or sponsors in areas in which it has special expertise.[7] The Office of Economic Opportunity has similarly demonstrated an ability to develop and manage a variety of internal and external research relationships and to apply knowledge so gained to improving standards of policy design and program implementation. Some interested agencies, however, have only recently emerged as important sponsors of social science research or have been slow to demonstrate a capacity for coordinated, cumulative development of research fields related to their respective missions. Still others have yet to perceive the importance of understanding the consequences of deficient social statistics for the day-to-day operation of their programs or for their long-range planning and policy development.

There are two practical reasons why this manifest disparity poses problems. In the first place, the Census Bureau is likely to be reluctant to delegate responsibility for funding research on the census to an agency that does not appear to subscribe to Bureau standards of project selection and supervision. More important, even if the Bureau were to agree to such a delegation of responsibility, taking the position, perhaps, that anyone who wants to study census problems

[7] See Advisory Committee on Government Programs in the Behavioral Sciences, National Research Council, *The Behavioral Sciences and the Federal Government* (Washington, D.C.: National Academy of Sciences), 1968, particularly p. 28.

should be encouraged to do so, it is not likely to accept the resulting research findings as readily as if they had emerged from projects that it had funded or administered directly.

Furthermore, there are many different kinds of research that need to be done. Different kinds of research competence are required for different kinds of studies and for different phases of some research projects. The range of needed knowledge and methodological training extends from those required for case analyses of statistical uses and error effects to ethnographic studies of the life ways of population subgroups. There are fundamental research undertakings that involve few researchers and have no necessary time constraints. There are areas of basic knowledge that urgently need to be explored because of their relevance to existing data-collection programs. There are, moreover, many projects that require close cooperation between statisticians and subject-matter specialists at every point from the initial stage of problem formulation to the final analysis and interpretation of research results.

Such diversity, in both substance and timing, places a premium on coherent, comprehensive research management. In order to make effective use of available research resources and to develop new capabilities that will be available at an appropriate moment in the future, careful attention must be paid to the cumulativeness of research findings over time and to the continuous development of substantive lines of research inquiry. A constant effort must be made to identify linkages among methodologically distinct projects and to stay abreast of the progress of research that, if not seemingly useful in the earlier stages of development, could eventually make significant contributions to the solution of important problems.

This kind of supervisory activity should not be entrusted to an agency or group of agencies with little or weak research management experience. It requires a clear locus of responsibility for substantive coordination of the several federal programs of social data collection and their associated research activities. It requires, in effect, a set of interagency relationships that does not exist at the present time.

The Office of Management and Budget (OMB) is responsible for administrative oversight of the federal statistical system. It sets standards of questionnaire design and scrutinizes all proposed data-collection efforts for such defects as unwarranted redundancy, irrelevance, and illegality. Through exercise of its budgetary authority, the Office maintains more than a modicum of control over agency operating and research programs. However, there is no staff capacity, either in the OMB or elsewhere in the federal system, for bringing together, organizing, and encouraging close cooperation among the disparate interests and resources that might be brought to bear on a problem like underenumeration.

The absence of such a coordinating capability is not necessarily to be lamented. As suggested in Chapter 3, one approach to resolving the multiagency research-participation problem would be to increase the Census Bureau research and development appropriation enough to permit the Bureau to develop the staff and external research capacity that would enable it to oversee and encourage the activities of other agencies supporting work in the area. Indeed, that option may be the easiest, and perhaps also the most effective, approach to research program development, given the present pattern of federal data collection and use relationships. Yet, since present budgetary constraints may make such a solution difficult at best, it would be well to search for other ways of bringing the relevant interests, resources, and research capabilities together.

One possibility would be to give the Office of Science and Technology the authority to coordinate census-related research sponsored by federal agencies and to give the National Science Foundation principal responsibility for direct support of fundamental research on problems of social data collection and use. The Office and the Foundation have already begun to move along those lines in the social-indicators field, where problems like underenumeration have potentially great significance. Moreover, since undercounting and other analogous data-gathering deficiencies appear to be related to a variety of social problems, the Foundation might find here yet another area in which fundamental research could be linked to important public policy issues.

Whatever new arrangements are created, they should be more imaginative and stronger than a heterogeneous interagency coordinating committee that meets infrequently, has no authority to develop research priorities, and tends to be informed of relevant work only after projects are already designed or under way. In fact, if responsibility for coordinating research on census deficiencies is given to a group as loosely structured and managed as the Federal Council on the 1970 Census,[8] it seems likely that little change will occur in the traditional manner of integrating relevant agency research efforts.

[8] In 1965, the Bureau of the Budget established a Federal Council on the 1970 Census to consider the proposed content of the 1970 Censuses of Population and Housing. Approximately 45 federal agencies designated representatives. However, the Council met infrequently and appears to have had little influence. Agency information needs were most often articulated in separate conversations

In organizational capacity and experience, the Census Bureau is among the most capable research institutions of the federal government. Hence, within a loosely structured interagency framework, the Bureau is very likely to emerge as the dominant figure, shaping the way census problems are viewed and advocating particular lines of research investment, thereby making it more difficult to achieve effective coordination of work that draws on the resources and points of view of the other interested parties.

Consider the situation: The Census Bureau has the strong advantage of an existing institutional research capability that, with the help of some of the better-developed statistical bureaus and offices in other federal agencies, would enable it to mount an effective program of research on social data collection and use problems. It presently lacks, however, the breadth of research perspective on social problems, the external ties, and the funding that would give such a program the requisite scope and depth. Other agencies, many of them dependent on census statistics, lack the Bureau's institutional research capacity but, by dint of their principal areas of research investment, have both funding and access to the kinds of perspectives and substantive knowledge resources that the Bureau needs. The central question is thus how best to enable the Bureau to develop a perspective that it does not now have, while at the same time encouraging agencies that have that perspective to become more conscious of its potential relevance to the problems they encounter as a consequence of deficiencies in the national social data base.

To achieve such an objective, the Bureau, for a time at least, may need to abjure the role of *primus inter pares* in the social statistics field. Problems like underenumeration are, in the final analysis, of greatest concern to census users, and the Census Bureau should, therefore, not be expected to assume total responsibility for resolving them. More important, however, the user agencies are more likely to cooperate and to support the Bureau in an environment that encourages pluralistic conceptions and approaches and where the important dimensions of problems are defined in ways that attend to the diverse policy and program responsibilities of the affected parties.

---

between the Census Bureau, the Bureau of the Budget, and heads of user agencies, See U.S. Congress, House of Representatives, Subcommittee on Census and Statistics of the Committee on Post Office and Civil Service, *Hearings on the 1970 Census and Legislation Related Thereto*, 91st Congress, 1st Session (Washington, D.C.: U.S. Government Printing Office), April–June 1969, pp. 13–14, 84.

Appendix A:
Principal Findings and Recommendations

Recommendation 1

Being able to answer the broad question of how much underenumeration is curable depends to a considerable extent on first being able to determine how much underenumeration is tolerable. To answer that question, however, it is essential to know in greater detail than present information allows how census data are actually used. Existing knowledge about census uses, while extensive, is scattered and incomplete. There is no current, comprehensive source or compilation of sources of descriptive information about even those uses of census data that are required by federal statute. Nor is a continuing systematic review of the end uses of census material now the responsibility of any established federal agency. *There should be a cumulative, up-to-date register of all statutory uses that are made of census data for the purpose of allocating government funds and developing basic social services, and the Census Bureau should take the lead in establishing such a list.* Moreover, the register should be gradually expanded in the direction of including all identifiable, official governmental uses of census statistics, beginning, for example, with those that are required by administrative order, regulation, or customary practice, supplemented, wherever feasible, by information on the kinds and frequency of uses made in the private sector of the economy and by individuals engaged in scientific research.

Recommendation 2

Compilation of a register of census uses will provide information about the range of purposes that official social statistics serve, but it will not offer more than impressionistic insights into the practical effects of incomplete or inaccurate census statistics on even those policy, decision-making, and research uses that can be readily identified. Accordingly, in addition to establishing and maintaining a register, *the Census Bureau and other interested departments and agencies (including those that are not prime statistics producers) should provide support for case studies of the manner in which census data are used in the statutory allocation of federal, state, and local revenues and of the changes in those allocations that would result from adjusting the data to account for various hypothesized rates of underenumeration.*

Recommendation 3

During the last two decades, the focus of the Census Research and Evaluation Programs has been defined by a desire to improve the overall quality of population census data. The Census Bureau has concentrated its efforts on achieving two principal objectives: making it possible to obtain an accurate count of the total population once every 10 years and establishing and improving the reliability and validity of items of information provided by persons counted or interviewed in censuses and current surveys. This strategic approach to census improvement has had important consequences. The Bureau has developed outstanding competence in such fields as statistics, demography, and social survey methods. It has pioneered significant advances in methods of data collection and analysis. However, the Bureau's attention has been sharply focused on one research instrument—the census questionnaire—and on one research framework—the various methods of delivering, retrieving, and interpreting completed census forms. Research and evaluation efforts in that context have produced important findings, most notably the sizable enumerator contribution to response variance. Yet, as the Bureau becomes increasingly concerned with the enumeration problems of small population subgroups, styles of problem definition and research design that have served it well in the past may become less productive of manageable solutions to census-taking deficiences. Accordingly, *in planning future research on underenumeration and other social data-gathering problems, more emphasis should be placed on developing new conceptual frameworks for the exploration of phenomena not usually perceived as relevant to the organized process of collecting census and survey information. Operationally, moreover, the Census Bureau should actively seek to broaden the base of social science knowledge and training to which it currently has access.*

Recommendation 4

The sponsors of census and census-related research should make a stronger commitment to continuing study of the social and social-psychological dimensions of population enumeration and description. That is, *the present conception of enumeration-related research should be expanded in ways that place greater stress on the relationship between census-taking problems, such as underenumeration, and the social contexts in which censuses and surveys are conducted.*

There is still insufficient evidence to warrant concluding that the majority of uncounted persons is to be found at one extreme of the economic spectrum, or to assert that being black makes a person less likely to be counted than, say, being poor, or functionally illiterate, or even moderately wealthy and very mobile. Several different factors are surely responsible for underenumeration. Hence, although the evidence of black undercoverage is dramatic, there is a need for research along other lines of investigation tied to different causal hypotheses. In particular, studies should be encouraged on such topics as

● Modes of social linkage within and among various social groups or categories and the effect of those linkages on social visibility, including studies of the ability of "insiders" to locate persons in such groups or categories

● Social organization and differentiation by life style, with particular emphasis on the effects of geographic and social mobility

● The relationship between life styles, life cycles, and conventional linkages to social institutions, including the role of ideologies in the maintenance or attenuation of such linkages

● The relationship between census and other standard demographic categories (for example, marital status, number of offspring, race, relationship to head) and the subjective categories used by members of specific subpopulations, such as ethnic subcultures, social dropouts, religious cults, migrants, and other marginal occupational groups

● Factors influencing decisions to participate or not to participate in sample surveys, including detailed analyses of the characteristics of dropouts from panel and list samples and longitudinal and epidemiological studies

• The social bases, rationales, and consequences of ideological and related forms of doctrinal opposition to aggregate information gathering by government and other public agencies

• Search methods of organizations routinely engaged in service or research activities that entail the location of "hard-to-find" populations—for example, welfare organizations, collection and credit agencies, market research operations that survey mobile populations, and organizations that compile registries of noncareer professionals, such as nurses, schoolteachers, and technicians

• Secondary analyses of social and behavioral science research findings related to the participation and compliance of populations in both voluntary and legally sanctioned governmental information-gathering activities (the Current Population Survey, public health surveys, municipal, state, and federal tax returns, various licensing and registration programs), as well as analyses of internal Census Bureau reports and documents bearing on problems of resistance, hostility, refusal, or other cases of inadequate response to census queries

Such a broad approach to census-taking problems has the disadvantage of diffuse formulation, but it offers the important benefit of suggesting many opportunities to develop new perspectives and conceptual frameworks for the exploration of phenomena not usually associated with social data deficiencies. Moreover, adopting an exploratory strategy that subjects the entire census-taking activity to a very broad critical examination and analysis is one of the best ways of enlisting the interest and cooperation of competent researchers who have not previously worked directly on census problems.

Recommendation 5

One relatively simple way of increasing the amount of attention given to the social aspects of enumeration problems would, of course, be to return to earlier research and evaluation studies in search of insights and explanations of why some procedural innovations may have been more effective than others. Certainly, that line of inquiry should be pursued. However, secondary analysis of findings produced with other research objectives in mind will not be sufficient alone. New projects will have to be initiated and new programmatic research commitments made in order to enlarge the variety of reasonable hypotheses and corroborative sources of information about the social dynamics of large-scale data-gathering efforts.

A number of ideas suggested by the conceptualization of census taking as a socially organized activity can be translated into research directly aimed at improving standard enumeration procedures. Others will require longer-term exploratory studies to develop additional evidence about the kinds of people who do not get counted, and how, and why. Research projects of both kinds should be undertaken. *In particular, it is recommended that*

  ● *Additional controlled experimental studies of questionnaire wordings and formats be used (a) to investigate further the influence on response patterns of such factors as race, sex, age, region, and social class, (b) to explore respondent interpretations of alternative renderings of census terms, and (c) to assess the advantages of translating entire questionnaires into other languages*
  ● *An effort be made to ascertain the usefulness of providing indigenous enumerators with an identity other than that of agents of the Census Bureau, including additional attention to the feasibility of hiring mailmen as follow-up enumerators*
  ● *The utility of communication research as an instrument for gaining a better understanding of the reasons for census and survey undercoverage be fully explored* [For example, there should be a nationwide study of attitudes toward privacy and anonymity; a survey to gain a better understanding of how the census is perceived; thorough pretesting of census public information material and media; content analysis of the national media effort; evaluation of the effects of census public information campaigns; and sufficient funds provided for such research to permit the purchase of advertising.]

In addition, there should be

  ● *Further study of the effects of calendar-related events on the census-taking process*
  ● *Continuing study of the perceptions and decision-making criteria that inform the editing of address registers by postal carriers, as well as additional, more intensive efforts to identify and describe the characteristics of persons who allegedly live at addresses at which mailmen find postal delivery especially difficult*
  ● *Further exploration of the possibility of making being counted*

in the census an individual responsibility, including cooperation among the several interested statistical agencies in undertaking both pilot studies to determine if information from registration systems could be used to make additional gains in census coverage and accuracy, and more frequent evaluation of the registration of vital events and of statistics on the number of individuals moving into and out of the country

● A series of small-scale exploratory comparisons between local record sources and census records, with the objective of identifying those record sources in which otherwise uncounted people might be found

● Additional casual interview studies in connection with special censuses or census pretests in areas that presented acute enumeration problems in 1970

● Cooperation between the Census Bureau and other interested federal agencies in developing a planned participant–observer research program designed to improve understanding of government social data needs, the impediments to collecting necessary information, and the difficulties involved in interpreting information that has been or could be collected

● An intensive survey of the difficulties encountered in conducting longitudinal studies by social scientists, the Census Bureau, and others; thorough analysis of the characteristics of dropouts from longitudinal studies; and modest longitudinal studies of groups drawn from populations that might be expected to prefer social invisibility.

Recommendation 6

In general, the Census Bureau has hesitated to make adjustments in direct counts for small geographic areas because of the large methodological problems involved and because of the damage that could be done by publication of seriously erroneous estimates. Census counts are an important part of the political process. In any disputed counting situation, there are likely to be special interests with a stake in having the official counts altered in one direction or another. Also, because of the interlocking structure of the federal statistical system, adjustments in the counts for one set of localities, or for one set of distributions in an official statistical series, might necessitate corresponding changes for other localities and for many other statistical series. There are, however, many census users with policy and program interests that are frustrated by the lack of reliable census counts or estimates for small areas. Hence, *increased support should be given to analytical studies of small-area underenumeration (as well as other sources of census error) with the objectives of (a) discovering which demographic, economic, and other characteristics of an area are associated with enumeration error and (b) devising methods for adjusting small-area census counts.*

Recommendation 7

It seems clear that the diversity of research activities and competence that would be required for a systematic attack on problems of census data collection and use points to a need for greater cooperation and coordination among the many potential sponsors of research on census and survey problems. In the present context of federal agency support for research on social problems, this suggests that *much stronger efforts should be made to join the kinds of social science competence found on the staff and in the external research communities of some of the principal social data users with the kinds of scientific expertise that has been well developed by the principal data producers.*

One possibility would be to give the Office of Science and Technology the authority to coordinate census-related research sponsored by federal agencies and to give the National Science Foundation principal responsibility for direct support of fundamental research on problems of social data collection and use. However, whatever new arrangements might be created, the user agencies will be more likely to cooperate in an environment that encourages pluralistic conceptions and approaches and where the important dimensions of problems are defined in ways that attend to the diverse policy and program responsibilities of the affected parties.

Appendix B:
City Characteristics and
Incomplete Census Responses[1]

In the autumn of 1969, the Advisory Committee established a Subcommittee on Data Analysis, which initiated an exploratory multiple regression analysis of several available measures of census enumeration difficulties in U.S. cities in 1960.[2] The immediate objective of the project was to identify relationships among certain city characteristics as explanatory (or independent) variables in a regression model in which one of several variables measuring enumeration difficulties (hereafter referred to as "response failure," or RF, variables) was the dependent variable. The ultimate objective of the work, however, was to determine whether it would be useful to explore further two hypotheses: that some city characteristics are strongly related to some RF variables; and that RF variables could be used as proxy measures for underenumeration. That is, the second hypothesis was that a city with a substantial amount of response failure would also be a city with a substantial amount of underenumeration, or, more technically, that RF and underenumeration are positively correlated.

[1] The work reported here is also discussed briefly in Chapter 7, pp. 107–109.
[2] The Subcommittee, composed of Professors Glen Cain, Reynolds Farley, and Leo Schnore, was responsible for the methodology of the research reported here and for selecting the variables to be analyzed. Almost all of the empirical work was carried out by Daniel Cumings, a graduate student at the University of Wisconsin, to whom the Advisory Committee wishes to express its gratitude for a job well done. Mr. Cumings wrote a report, "Underenumeration and Nonresponse and Their Ecological Correlates," January, 1970, which, along with further empirical and interpretative work by Subcommittee members using Cumings' data, has provided the material for this Appendix. Cumings' unpublished paper is available from the Division of Behavioral Sciences of the National Research Council.

It was, of course, also hoped that the project, if successful, could be used to suggest improvements in census enumeration procedures. By identifying characteristics of cities that were strongly related to response failures in 1960, characteristics such as educational attainment or a particular age composition, the Census Bureau might have had a firmer base for selecting intensive enumeration procedures and areas in 1970.

It is important to note that the regression analyses undertaken provide only indirect, weak tests of the two hypotheses. Investigating the second hypothesis, for example, consisted of determining whether city characteristics believed to be indicative of (or correlated with) underenumeration—characteristics such as the age, sex, race, and socioeconomic composition of a city—would also be found to be significantly[3] related to the RF variables. Although the hypothesized statistical relation between RF variables and those characteristics believed to be sources of underenumeration *was* found, as reported below, there is neither sufficient supplementary verification nor enough knowledge about how accurately the relation is measured from the exploratory work undertaken to accept the hypothesis with confidence. Hence, the positive findings should be viewed only as justifying further research.

Data and Variables Used

In the final report of the 1960 Census, there are 21 variables for urban places of 10,000 inhabitants or more that define various types of nonresponse and imputations for nonresponse.[4] Three of the variables were selected as dependent variables for the regression analyses:

---

[3] Note that the terms "significantly related" and "strongly related" are often used loosely and should not be taken to imply the use of formal rules of hypothesis testing or other rigorously developed criteria. In the discussion of Tables B-1 and B-2, the Subcommittee has adopted the convention of referring to variables as "statistically significant," whose *t*-ratios (ratio of the regression coefficient to its standard error) are larger than 1.645. The Subcommittee recognizes, however, that there are numerous reasons to question both the meaning of "statistical significance" and the use of the criterion in this context. Yet, by emphasizing the preliminary, exploratory nature of the analysis, it is hoped that immediate demands for more rigorous procedures might be forestalled.

[4] U.S. Bureau of the Census, *U.S. Census of Population, 1960: Final Report* PC (1)-B, and PC (1)-C for each state (Washington, D.C.: U.S. Government Printing Office), 1961 and 1962, Tables B–2 and C–3.

• The percentage of the population imputed because of noninterview (hereafter referred to as NONINTVW)

• The percentage of the population with one or more imputations for items asked in the 100 percent census count (hereafter referred to as ONEPLUS)

• The percentage of the population in the 25 percent sample with unacceptable entries in two or more sample items (hereafter referred to as SMPLINFO)

A fourth variable (SUM/NONRESPONSE) was created to illustrate and test the use of a linear combination of RF variables. It represents the sum of NONINTVW, ONEPLUS, and SMPLINFO.

The units of observation for the analyses were 653 (out of a total of 675) cities of 25,000 inhabitants or more, for which a large number of demographic and socioeconomic variables thought to be associated with underenumeration were conveniently accessible in secondary sources.[5] A full list of variable definitions will be found in Table B-1. The variables selected obviously do not constitute a definitive list. Rather, they reflect a judgment that, because the unenumerated population is disproportionately black, male, and between 18 and 35 years old, underenumeration is more likely to occur in the inner zones of cities, in rural areas, among the poor, the uneducated, among migrants (or other transient groups), among roomers, boarders, the unmarried, and probably, therefore, among persons employed in low-paying, high-turnover occupations.

Moreover, many of the independent variables are highly intercorrelated. For example, four variables (MEDSCHOL, UNDE5E, PHS, and PCTCOLLG) all measure the level of educational attainment in the city. Hence, if all or most of the variables were used in a single

---

[5] Data for all variables, except INDEPCTY, CENTCITY, SUBURB, and MANUFACT, were found in the U.S. Bureau of the Census, *County and City Data Book 1962* (Washington, D.C.: U.S. Government Printing Office), 1962, Table 6. Data for INDEPCTY, CENTCITY, SUBURB, and MANUFACT were found in *The Municipal Year Book 1967* (Chicago: International City Managers Association), 1967, Table 1. A separate set of regressions was run for 288 cities for which the closing date of the district census office (hereafter referred to as CLOSEDAY) was available from unpublished Census Bureau sources. This variable could be regarded as another measure of enumeration problems. The later the closing date, presumably, the greater the difficulty. The variable was used as an additional predictor, or explanatory, variable in the separate set of regressions and was, in fact, found to be positively correlated with RF variables. The regression results in which CLOSEDAY was used are not reported here.

TABLE B-1   Acronyms, Definitions, Means,[a] and Standard Deviations[a]
of Variables Used in the Analyses

Acronyms	Definitions	Mean	Standard Deviation
NONINTVW	Percent of population substituted for omissions due to noninterview	408–3	235–3
ONEPLUS	Percent of population of the 100 percent count with one or more allocations	302–2	116–2
SMPLINFO	Percent of population in the 25 percent sample with unacceptable entries in two or more sample characteristics	150–2	983–3
POP	Total population	115+3	377+3
DENSITY	Persons per square mile	544+1	437+1
POPCHANG	Percent population change 1950–1960	500–1	109+0
NW1960	Percent nonwhite	101–1	124–1
CHANGENW	Percent nonwhite in 1960 minus percent nonwhite in 1950	124–2	387–2
GROUPS	Percent living in group quarters	303–2	404–2
UNDER5	Percent under 5 years of age	111–1	207–2
P21	Percent 21 years and older	615–1	467–2
P65	Percent 65 years and older	942–2	339–2
FOREIGN	Percent foreign-born	602–2	490–2
FRGNPRNT	Percent native, of foreign or mixed parentage	155–1	101–1
PCTCOPLS	Percent married	229–1	814–2
NOHHLDS	Percent of married couples without their own households	203–2	947–3
MEDINCOM	Median family income	618+1	134+1
M3000	Percent of families with income under $3,000	167–1	836–2
MEDSCHOL	For the population 25 years and older, median school years completed	111–1	119–2
UNDE5E	For the population 25 years and older, percent completing less than five years of school	702–2	488–2
PHS	Percent completing high school or more	456–1	114–1
PCTCOLLG	Percent of total population enrolled in college	254–2	432–2
SAMEHOUS	Percent of residents over 5 years old in the same house in 1960 as in 1955	472–1	984–2
DIFFCNTY	Percent of current residents living in a different county in 1955	185–1	104–1
PCTLBRFR	Percent of population in the civilian labor force	399–1	385–2
UNEMPLOY	Percent of labor force unemployed	505–2	183–2
PCTMALE	Percent of labor force male	646–1	405–2
INDEPCTY	Score 1 if an independent city is not in a Standard Metropolitan Statistical Area (SMSA), 0 otherwise	240–3	428–3
SUBURB	Score 1 if a suburb, 0 otherwise	345–3	476–3
CENTCITY	Score 1 if a central city in an SMSA, 0 otherwise	415–3	493–3
MANUFACT	Percent of city economy devoted to manufacturing	425–1	206–1
WHCOLLAR	Percent employed persons in white-collar occupations	464–1	926–2
ONEUNIT	Percent of housing units in one-unit structures	703–1	190–1
P101	Percent of occupied units with more than 1.01 persons per room	982–2	482–2
DIFFUNIT	Percent of occupied units moved into during 1958–1960	341–1	867–2

TABLE B-1   (Continued)

Acronyms	Definitions	Mean	Standard Deviation
PCTOWNER	Percent of housing units owner-occupied	601–1	134–1
PCTGOVT	Percent of total population working for the city government	113–2	645–3
LOGPOP	Logarithm of population	110–1	842–3
LOGDEN	Logarithm of density	839–2	657–3

[a]Here, $a + b$ means $a(10^b)$ and $a - b$ means $a(10^{-b})$. Thus, in the column for "Mean" and the row for "POP," 115+3 means $115(10^3) = 155,000$, and in the column for "Standard Deviation," and row for "P21," 467–2 means $467(10^{-2}) = 4.67$.

regression, their high degree of multicollinearity could be expected to cause the estimated regression coefficients to be highly unstable and difficult to interpret. For this reason, a procedure was sometimes adopted that consisted of retaining only statistically significant variables for some of the regressions.

Results of the Regression Analyses

The conventional assumptions[6] regarding the use of regression analysis are not fully satisfied, so the results should be interpreted with caution. Table B-2 shows a regression in which most of the independent variables are included. It was usually found that as few as six variables explained most (approximately 75 percent) of the total amount of variation explainable by all the variables.

The dependent variable for the regression shown in Table B-2 is NONINTVW—the percentage of the population imputed for omissions due to noninterview. Similar results were obtained, but are not reported, for other dependent variables. Only a few comments will be made about Table B-2. First, about 40 percent of the variation in the dependent variable could be attributed to the model—representing an R^2 that is overwhelmingly significantly different from zero in the statistical sense (given the assumptions underlying the analysis), although the criteria for assessing its practical significance are lacking. Second, the signs on the coefficients generally agree with the expectations that guided the choice of variables to be included in the model. Thus, NW1960, the percentage of the city's population that

[6]N. R. Draper and H. Smith, *Applied Regression Analysis* (New York: John Wiley & Sons, Inc.), 1966, p. 17.

was nonwhite, has a positive sign, indicating that the higher the percentage nonwhite, the greater the response failure. However, although NW1960 had the second highest simple correlation (not shown) with NONINTVW, when all the remaining variables were entered—many being strongly correlated with NW1960—the statistical significance of the NW1960 effect diminished to a "low" level.

TABLE B-2 Multiple Regression: The Dependent Variable Is the Percentage of the Population Imputed Due to Noninterviews (653 Cities)

Independent Variable	Regression Coefficient[a]	t Ratio
CENTCITY	.232–1	.958
CHANGENW	.114–1	4.802
DIFFCNTY	−.552–3	−.348
DIFFUNIT	.624–2	2.366
FOREIGN	.155–3	.096
GROUPS	−.614–2	−1.625
INDEPCTY	−.481–1	−1.906
LOGDEN	.188–1	1.227
LOGPOP	.320–1	2.407
M3000	.524–2	1.516
MANUFACT	−.361–4	−.069
MEDINCOM	−.146–4	−.866
MEDSCHOL	−.237–1	−1.036
NOHHLDS	.980–2	.793
NW1960	.127–2	1.102
ONEUNIT	−.136–2	−1.135
P21	.216–1	3.574
P65	−.319–2	−.603
P101	.141–1	3.886
PCTCOLLG	−.191–2	−.550
PCTCOPLS	−.134–2	−1.420
PCTGOVT	.265–1	1.727
PCTLBRFR	−.660–2	−1.611
PCTMALE	.420–3	.114
PCTOWNER	.265–2	1.559
PHS	.592–2	2.168
POPCHANG	.834–4	.926
SAMEHOUS	−.213–2	−.993
UNDE5E	−.330–2	−.793
UNDER5	−.172–1	−1.729
UNEMPLOY	.114–2	.204
WHCOLLAR	−.107–2	−.503
Constant	−1.24	−1.948

Estimated standard deviation of residuals: .19
Goodness of fit: R^2=.41, R=.64

[a]The style of notation used here is the same as in Table B-1. See the explanatory footnote to Table B-1.

The change in the percentage nonwhite from 1950 to 1960 (CHANGNW) was also significantly and positively related to NONINTVW at each stage of the regression. The positive sign agrees with the *a priori* speculation that growth in the nonwhite population, particularly if it reflected in-migration of young adult black males, would be positively related to response failure (and, therefore, to underenumeration). The quantitative magnitude of the effect of CHANGNW does not seem large, however. The regression coefficient indicates that a one-point change in this variable (defined as the percentage change in the proportion nonwhite from 1950 to 1960) is associated with a .01 change in NONINTVW. To make this clearer, consider that the mean value of NONINTVW is 0.41%, that the mean value of CHANGNW is 1.23 percentage points, and that the regression coefficient of CHANGNW is .011. Thus, a change in the latter from 1.23 to 2.23 would bring about an expected increase in NONINTVW from 0.41 percent to 0.42 percent. The lowest value of CHANGNW was –19 percentage points, and the largest value was +35 percentage points. A 10-point change would not be unusual, therefore, and this amount of change would be associated with an increase in NONINTVW of, say, 0.41 percent to 0.52 percent.

The percentage of the population over age 21 (P21) is a third variable that was positively related to NONINTVW—an expected result if the percentage in the largest underenumerated age groups (20–35) were positively correlated with P21.[7] Similarly, the variable M3000—a crude index of poverty—has its expected positive sign, and, as further analysis showed, the only reason the variable is not of greater statistical significance is that it is so highly correlated with median income (MEDINCOM) and other economic variables. This is an important point to make. The lack of statistical significance on many of the variables (such as M3000) should *not* be viewed as an indication that the conceptual variable they represent (in this case, low income) is unrelated to the dependent variable.

There is no need to observe here the sign of each variable, noting its expected sign, and discussing the quantitative magnitude of the regression coefficient and its significance level. Suffice it to say that among the statistically significant variables (that is, those with *t*-ratios over 1.645), CHANGNW, P21, P101, DIFFUNIT, and LOGPOP all

---

[7] Note that the effect of P21 is observed holding constant the effects of the percentage of the population under 5 and over 65. Unfortunately, the data sources used did not permit finer age breakdowns.

had the "correct" sign. Only PHS (percentage completing high school) was completely unexpected in its effect (being *positively* related to NONINTVW); and PCTGOVT and UNDER5 were ambiguous. Moreover, when regressions such as that shown in Table B-2 were fit with each of the other dependent variables defined in Table B-1, the results were generally similar with respect to signs of the independent variable and the percentage of variance explained (R^2).

Another set of regressions was run with the 288 cities for which CLOSEDAY—the closing date of the district census office—was available. Still others were fit for cities of over and under 100,000 population. In the latter—the regressions for different-sized cities— somewhat better results were obtained, using as a criterion a smaller estimate of the standard deviation of residuals, but the overall results in all the regressions with a smaller number of cities were similar to those already reported for the 653 others.

Implications

The reported regression analyses of city characteristics and response failure variables represent a strategy for research more than a block of substantive findings. If the method appears worthwhile, the analysis could be extended in a number of different directions. For example, it could be applied to different areal units of observation, such as cities stratified by size and type, counties, or census tracts. It could include other ecological variables (more precisely measured it is to be hoped), such as more finely defined age and ethnic groups. It could be used for evaluating field procedures and, if supplementary information should appear to warrant such an extension, for measuring underenumeration. Moreover, since it would be desirable to adopt the last-mentioned variant of the strategy in the context of a controlled experimental design, the type of research reported here, with existing data, could also provide information that would be useful in formulating such evaluation designs—for example, which sample stratifications and "control variables" would be advantageous?

It is difficult, however, to assess the substantive findings of the Subcommittee project in terms of the ultimate objectives initially stated: to determine (a) whether some city characteristics might be strongly related to response failure, (b) whether response failure variables might serve as proxies for underenumeration, and (c) whether, if those tests were passed, ecological variables could be identified that would suggest ways of improving census procedures. In support of the critical hypothesis—namely, that RF variables could be used as proxies for underenumeration—are the agreements in sign of the effects of various independent variables believed to be related to both underenumeration and response failure. Yet there were also effects of a few variables that had signs opposite to those expected. Moreover, systematic analysis is necessary to determine whether the quantitative magnitudes of the reported effects, and their levels of significance, are to be judged as supporting even the first hypothesis.

The current state of theoretical and empirical knowledge is too weak to serve as a guide in determining which variables provide the more critical tests of the hypothesized relationships. Similarly, the lack of a theoretical framework for specifying the "causes" of underenumeration (or even of response failure) does not permit a judgment as to whether the explanatory power of the analysis is sufficiently strong to be useful for scientific or policy purposes. Hence, the test of whether this line of research may produce more conclusive results depends on the willingness of the research community interested in census and survey procedures to carry the analysis forward.

Appendix C:
Annotated Bibliography:
Analytic Methods for Estimation
of Underenumeration

This is a working bibliography and is surely not complete. The items and comments reflect the reading, thinking, and discussion that led to Chapter 6. Items are arranged alphabetically by author. The lengths and amounts of detail in the commentaries do not necessarily indicate a judgment with regard to the overall significance of the separate articles or books.

Akers, Donald S. "Immigration Data and National Population Estimates for the United States," *Demography*, 4 (1967), 262–272.
From the summary:

> The immigration component in national population estimates is comparatively small, but it is not insignificant and may indeed be an important source of error. Therefore, it warrants the consideration of those concerned with population estimates. The paper considers alternative methods for deriving estimates of immigration . . . from 1950 to 1965. They are developed from estimates previously published by the Bureau of the Census, but they differ at some points where new data have become available or where a review of the data has led to a change in judgment on how best to use them. The paper also presents suggestions on how immigration statistics might be altered for purposes of improving the estimates.

Also, see p. 267 *ff.* about deficiencies in migration data (affecting demographic accounting).

Bogue, Donald J., and Beverly Duncan. "A Composite Method for Estimating Post-censal Population of Small Areas by Age, Sex, and Color," in U.S. Department of Health, Education, and Welfare, Public Health Service, National Office of Vital Statistics, *Vital Statistics Special Reports, Selected Studies 47* (August 24, 1959), 161–185.
Uses local census results; local birth, death, and school registration data both at time of census and after; United States census data as well as national postcensal estimates; United States birth, death, and school registration data both at time of census and after. Method particularly weak on young adult males. Can this method based on census data ever give better results than the census? No model making or error analysis was attempted.

Bogue, Donald J., Bhaskar D. Misra, and D. P. Dandekar. "A New Estimate of the Negro Population and Negro Vital Rates in the United States, 1930–1960," *Demography*, 1 (1964), 339–358.
The underenumeration errors given here are smaller than the 1950 values of Coale (1955). See Zelnik (1965).

Bogue, Donald J., and Edmund M. Murphy. "The Effect of Classification Errors upon Statistical Inferences: A Case Analysis with Census Data," *Demography*, 1 (1964), 42–55.
From the conclusion:

> The above exploration has succeeded, we hope, in emphasizing the importance of study of errors of classification. The results obtained here suggest most strongly that the correlation of the errors in direction and degree can powerfully affect the inferences drawn. Second, these results underline and support the principle that it is of utmost importance to reduce not only net errors but gross errors in all types of data-collecting because the pattern of association between gross errors has such a substantial effect upon inference.
>
> The study of error is a relatively recent development. We can only hope that this paper emphasizes anew the importance of these studies. No one would accept a sample estimate that did not include an estimate of the sampling error involved. We believe that the same criterion should be applied to errors of classification, where these can be measured.
>
> We recommend that every census tabulation should be covered by an estimate of the effects of error involved not only in terms of simple marginal distributions but also upon statistical inferences derived from cross-tabulations. It is hoped that the 1970 Census plans will include a renewed effort to reduce gross as well as net error. It is also hoped that private research organizations will conduct studies of this problem, using their field studies to obtain data.

Coale, Ansley J. "The Population of the United States in 1950 Classified by Age, Sex, and Color—A Revision of Census Figures," *Journal of the American Statistical Association*, 50 (1955), 16–54.
This is truly a central paper and has served as a point of departure for additional work.

Most computations, presented graphically and in tabular form, are very involved:

    a. Complete details not presentable

    b. Many sources for alternative explanations

    c. Arithmetic procedures accumulate errors. Propagation of error analysis begun but no statistical analysis attempted

    d. Variations in models for ease of computation cause substantial changes in computed results—lack of robustness

Most direct evidence in Figures 1 and 2 of age–color–sex ratios:

    a. Figures 1 and 2 not consistent and tabular values not given

    b. Large sex ratios for older ages suggest another major nonenumeration or inconsistency in the data

Age ratios adjusted for cohort size (Figure 3) do *not* pick out the nonenumeration evidence of working-age nonwhite males.

Table 5, using 1940 draft data, gives very strong evidence about nonenumeration of young adult males, particularly nonwhites, but for 1950 and 1960, see Siegel and Irwin (1969).

This study has been repeated and modified; see Heer (Ed.) (1968), particularly, the first chapter and the appendix.

Farley, Reynolds. " The Quality of Demographic Data for Nonwhites," *Demography*, 5 (1968), 1–10.
The young adult sex ratio for nonwhites is declining into the 1960's (see p. 5 and footnote 23). Enumeration difficulties might have perceptible, but not material, effects on demographic rates. Also discusses checking procedures, specifically including those discussed in U.S. Bureau of the Census (1964b).

Farley, Reynolds. *Growth of the Black Population.* Chicago: Markham (1970). 268 pp.
This book traces the growth of the black population throughout the nineteenth and twentieth centuries. It includes discussions of census undercount and presents some calculations that attempt to measure the effects of errors in census data.

Freytag, Hans Ludwig. "Statistische Probleme Einer Systematischen Beobachtung der Bevölkerungsbewegung–Das Konzept der Demographischen Gesamtrechnung," *Allgemeines Statistisches Archiv*, 53 (1969), 329–345.
English abstract of this paper on *demographic accounting* on p. 345. Footnotes contain additional bibliography. The concept of demographic accounting here includes that of the present report, but is much more far-reaching. See Stone, Stone, and Gunton (1968) and Stone (1971).

Goldberg, David, V. R. Rao, and N. K. Namboodiri. "A Test of the Accuracy of Ratio Correlation Population Estimates," *Land Economics*, 40 (1964), 100–102.
In this paper the regression technique is shown off to positive advantage.

The article examines multiple regression for 1950/1940 Michigan county population ratios on corresponding ratios for seven "independent" variates from births to sales tax. It then applies the resulting prediction equation (and a truncated version thereof) to the 1960/1950 population changes and compares multiple regression with some other approaches, to the advantage of the former.

The errors of estimation are examined by giving frequencies of absolute error in three classes and giving average absolute error. More detail is desirable–for example, the signed errors, some graphs, including bivariate graphs, dependence between the errors of different methods.

One worries about consistency of aggregation whenever a method based on ratios (or anything else nonlinear) is used in this kind of context. To be specific, suppose that P_{t+1} and P_t are populations of a county at two successive time points and that we estimate the former by

$$\hat{P}_{t+1} = \left(a + b \, \frac{x_{t+1}}{x_t} \right) P_t,$$

where a and b are constants from prior experience and x_{t+1}, x_t are values of one (for simplicity) independent variate, say births. Now suppose we do the same thing for a contiguous county, using primes for its P's and x's,

$$\hat{P}'_{t+1} = \left(a + b \, \frac{x'_{t+1}}{x'_t} \right) P'_t.$$

Then $\hat{P}_{t+1} + \hat{P}'_{t+1}$ is the estimated $t + 1$ population for the two counties together.

On the other hand, it might be just as reasonable to estimate the population of the two counties by

$$\left(a + b \; \frac{x_{t+1} + x'_{t+1}}{x_t + x'_t} \right) (P_t + P'_t),$$

which will not be the same in general. One might object that, for pairs of counties, a and b should change, but carrying out the whole procedure, including computation of a and b by county pairs, will not solve the consistency problem.

See Rosenberg (1968) and Pursell (1970) for further developments.

Heer, David M. (Ed.). *Social Statistics and the City (Report of a Conference Held in Washington, D.C., June 22-23, 1967)*. Cambridge, Massachusetts: Harvard University Press for the Joint Center for Urban Studies of the Massachusetts Institute of Technology and Harvard University (1968). 186 pp.

Contents
> Foreword—Daniel P. Moynihan
> Introduction—David M. Heer
> 1. Completeness of Coverage of the Nonwhite Population in the 1960 Census and Current Estimates, and Some Implications—Jacob S. Siegel
> 2. Procedural Difficulties in Taking Past Censuses in Predominantly Negro, Puerto Rican, and Mexican Areas—Leon Pritzker and N. D. Rothwell
> 3. Needed Innovations in 1970 Census Data Collection Procedures: A Census View—Conrad Taeuber
> 4. Needed Improvements in Census Data Collection Procedures with Special Reference to the Disadvantaged—Everett S. Lee
> 5. Vital Statistics for the Negro, Puerto Rican, and Mexican Populations: Present Quality and Plans for Improvement—Robert D. Grove
> 6. Needed Statistics for Minority Groups in Metropolitan Areas—Daniel O. Price
> Appendix: An Evaluation of Coverage in the 1960 Census of Population by Techniques of Demographic Analysis and by Composite Methods—Jacob S. Siegel and Melvin Zelnik
> Resolutions of the Conference
> List of Conference Participants

From page 31:

> In view of the omission of one out of four nonwhite males aged 20–39 in the CPS in 1965 and in view of the considerable effort and care that have gone into the design and conduct of the CPS, it is clearly extremely difficult to achieve even a fair level of coverage of this group in particular, and of nonwhites in general, in even a very carefully designed and executed sample survey.

From page 66:

> Seven out of ten white persons but fewer than three out of ten nonwhites who were missed in the 1960 Census were subsequently found in missed quarters by post-enumeration survey interviewers. Thus, a minority of white people but a large majority of nonwhites who were missed in 1960 were either present but unreported in enumerated living quarters or were not staying in any kind of place covered by the census.

Johnston, Denis F., and James Wetzel. "Effect of the Census Undercount on Labor Force Estimates," *Monthly Labor Review*, 92 (1969), 3–13. (Reprint No. 2609 and Special Labor Force Report No. 105.)

Labor force utilization rates are substantially changed depending on whether or not they are computed with an allocation of the undercount. The small changes in rates between variations in allocation methods should not affect policy decisions or scientific inferences.

Marks, Eli S., and Joseph Waksberg. "Evaluation of Coverage in the 1960 Census of the Population through Case-by-Case Checking," *Proceedings of the Social Statistics Section of the American Statistical Association* (1966), 62–70.

From page 66:

> In comparing the reinterview results with those from demographic analyses, it can be seen that there is a moderately good correspondence for white females. We take this fact as evidence that these estimates are fairly reliable. There are very large discrepancies, however, for white males, nonwhite females and nonwhite males. With respect to the differences in age distributions, there are reasons to feel that the reinterview results are better in the upper ranges (65 and over). In the lower ranges (under age 15), the figures based on demographic analysis are undoubtedly superior. The reinterview results are also deficient for nonwhite adult males, and this group is probably the one most seriously understated in the reinterview approach. For the other population groups, there is considerable uncertainty as to which source is more accurate.

Price, Daniel O. "A Check on Underenumeration in the 1940 Census," *American Sociological Review,* 12 (1947), 44–49.

For 1940, draft data are a powerful check on nonenumeration by states. But see Siegel and Irwin (1969).

Price, Daniel O. *Changing Characteristics of the Negro Population.* (A 1960 Census Monograph.) Washington, D.C.: U.S. Government Printing Office (1969). 259 pp.

The effects of underenumeration on the apparent structure of the changes in the Negro population are discussed on pp. 15, 44, 122, 221, and 239.

Pursell, Donald E. "Improving Population Estimates with the Use of Dummy Variables," *Demography,* 7 (1970), 87–91.

Rosenberg, Harry. "Improving Current Population Estimates through Stratification," *Land Economics,* 44 (1968), 331–338.

Siegel, Jacob S. See Heer (Ed.) (1968).

Seigel, Jacob S. "Some Principles and Methods of Projections of Urban-Rural Population by Age and Sex," WPC/WP/436, *United Nations World Population Conference, Belgrade, August 30–September 10, 1965,* 91–96.

From page 91:

> Population projections may be viewed as approximations of probable future population size and changes resulting from various stated assumptions. In view of the considerable uncertainty regarding future changes in the urban–rural sectors, it is desirable to develop a set of several projections employing alternative assumptions with regard to the various components, particularly those which show great variation or uncertainty and potentially great impact on population size. The components vary with the method chosen. It is recommended that the principal series of projections employ only probable or realistically possible assumptions so that, as a set, the projections give an indication of the range in which the future size and age-sex distribution of the urban and rural populations will very probably fall. Such projections are not to be interpreted as predictions even though realistic approximations to future population size are sought. In fact, projections may be rendered seriously inadequate as predictions if, on the basis of the figures, the national plan specifically attempts to modify the course of regional growth to achieve preset national goals. Although planners tend to prefer only a single series of projections, it is more realistic to recognize the very wide range of uncertainty in urban-rural projections and to reflect it in the projections prepared. Furthermore, a "medium" or "most probable" series may best be avoided as prediction in a special guise. Accordingly, an even number (e.g., four) of principal series of projections are recommended; this does not preclude the preparation of additional "analytic" series for interpretative purposes, however.

Siegel, Jacob S., and Donald S. Akers. "Outlook for Population at Mid-Decade," *Proceedings of the Business and Economic Statistics Section of the American Statistical Association* (1965), 358–366.

From page 358:

> The most serious difficulties pertain to the projections of children, the persons born after the base date of the projections. Since for this segment of the population the projections are built up wholly on assumptions not only of mortality and immigration but of fertility as well, they are subject to far greater error than the projections of the population alive at the start of the period. For many purposes, however, as for projections of households, labor force, and so on, these do not become important until 15 or so years hence.

Of course, the projection errors will contain a component from census errors, including those of underenumeration.

Siegel, Jacob S., and Richard Irwin. "Annual Comparisons of Census and Selective Service Data, 1949–1968," *Social Biology*, 16 (1969), 109–114.

Apparently, the data from the Selective Service are not useful after 1940.

From page 110:

> Our comparison of the two series of data suggests that the degree of under-registration in the Selective Service figures is roughly equivalent to the degree of underenumeration inherent in the census figures underlying the corresponding intercensal and postcensal population estimates.

Siegel, Jacob S., and Melvin Zelnik. See Heer (Ed.) (1968).

Starsinic, Donald E., and Meyer Zitter. "Accuracy of the Housing Unit Method in Preparing Population Estimates for Cities," *Demography*, 5 (1968), 475–484.

Possibly useful material for development of regression methods.

Stone, Richard. *Demographic Accounting and Model-Building*. Paris: Organisation for Economic Cooperation and Development (1971). 125 pp. + tables.

Demographic accounting has been developed for several reasons. For our purposes, the accounts give a variety of arithmetic identities that must be satisfied by the flows of people. When the recorded data do not satisfy these identities, some enumeration difficulty—frequently underenumeration—has occurred. These techniques are in the same spirit as those of Coale (1955). See Freytag (1969) and Stone, Stone, and Gunton (1968).

Stone, Richard, Giovanna Stone, and Jane Gunton. "An Example of Demographic Accounting: The School Ages," *Minerva*, 6 (1968), 185–212.

This is a recent representative of a sequence of papers on demographic and economic accounting by Richard Stone and his co-workers at the University of Cambridge. See Freytag (1969) and Stone (1971).

Taeuber, Conrad, and Morris H. Hansen. "A Preliminary Evaluation of the 1960 Censuses of Population and Housing," *Proceedings of the Social Statistics Section of the American Statistical Association* (1963), 1–18.

One other published paper is related to this in ways we do not fully understand. It has the same authors and the same title. It appeared in *Demography*, 1 (1964), 1–14, and its first footnote says that it is a condensed version of a paper given at the meetings of the Population Association of America, Philadelphia, April 26, 1963.

U.S. Bureau of the Census "Infant Enumeration Study: 1950," *Procedural Studies of the 1950 Censuses.* Washington, D.C.: U.S. Government Printing Office (1953). 70 pp.

If the infant is missing, then it is very likely the rest of the family was missing because the enumerator did not locate the household.

U.S. Bureau of the Census. *Tract Data Compared for a 25 Percent Sample in a Complete Census.* Working Paper No. 3. Washington, D.C.: U.S. Government Printing Office (1956). 30 pp.

From page 1:

> By and large it appears that the sample will serve most purposes that would be served by the complete census. It is necessary to recognize, in this connection, that the complete census is subject to response errors, and that any uses requiring highly precise figures for small areas may not be served by either the sample or the complete census.

The implications of this statement have not yet been supported.

U.S. Bureau of the Census. *Local Population Estimates Prepared by State and City Agencies: Mail Survey of 1960.* Current Population Reports, Series P-25, No. 224. Washington, D.C.: U.S. Government Printing Office (1962). 16 pp.

This is a survey of the work being done at the state and local level. The practicalities of what the local people are doing, of course, will affect the kinds of estimates that are finally prepared at the local level.

U.S. Bureau of the Census. *Evaluation and Research Program of the U.S. Censuses of Population and Housing, 1960: Accuracy of Data on Population Characteristics as Measured by Reinterviews.* Series ER 60, No. 4. Washington, D.C.: U.S. Government Printing Office (1964a). 23 pp.

U.S. Bureau of the Census. *Evaluation and Research Program of the U.S. Censuses of Population and Housing, 1960: Accuracy of Data on Population Characteristics as Measured by CPS-Census Match.* Series ER 60, No. 5. Washington, D.C.: U.S. Government Printing Office (1964b). 58 pp.

Of the nonwhite sample in age group 25 to 34, it was found that 68 percent could be located in the census and had the same classification (Table 6). This suggests that counts such as age × sex × race × state would have substantial errors from measurement other than enumeration.

U.S. Bureau of the Census. *Evaluation and Research Program of the U.S. Censuses of Population and Housing, 1960: Record Check Studies of Population Coverage. Series* ER 60, No. 2. Washington, D.C.: U.S. Government Printing Office (1964c). 9 pp.

Samples of enumerated 1950, children born 1950-1960, people found in PES 1950 not in 1950 Census, and aliens. Except for excellent matching of aliens, the matching process was off by at least 9 percent (Table A).

It might be wise to pick the record check sample for 1980 prior to 1980—begin in 1970—and unobtrusively attempt to keep track of the sample.

U.S. Bureau of the Census. *Estimates of the Population of the United States and Components of Change, by Age, Color, and Sex, 1950 to 1960.* Current Pop-

ulation Reports, Series P–25, No. 310, by J. S. Siegel, D. S. Akers, and W. D. Jones. Washington, D.C. (1965a). 56 pp.
Comparisons of estimates based on different data (Appendix A) and ways of allocating undercount (Appendix C) are made.

U.S. Bureau of the Census. *National Census Survival Rates, by Color and Sex for 1950 to 1960.* Current Population Reports, Series P–23, No. 15. Washington, D.C. (1965b). 11 pp.
Details for constructing and using these rates are given. This report illustrates the auditing method with just a slight amount of model making.

U.S. Bureau of the Census. *Methods of Population Estimation: Part 1 – Illustrative Procedure on the Census Bureau's Component Method II.* Current Population Reports, Series P–25, No. 339. Washington, D.C. (1966a). 17 pp.
Details are given of an accounting method.

U.S. Bureau of the Census. *Estimates of the Population of States: July 1, 1965 with Provisional Estimates for July, 1966.* Current Population Reports, Series P–25, No. 348. Washington, D.C. (1966b). 15 pp.
Uses two procedures and averages.

U.S. Bureau of the Census. *Use of Internal Revenue Service Data for Preparing Small-Area Population Estimates,* PA-(57) (January 12), and *Further Experimentation with IRS Data for Small-Area Population Estimates,* PA-(64) (September 25). Washington, D.C. (1968a).
Auxiliary variables and regression methods are used in population estimation.

U.S. Bureau of the Census. *The Current Population Survey Reinterview Program, January 1961 through December 1966.* Technical Paper 19. Washington, D.C.: U.S. Government Printing Office (1968b). 60 pp.
Table 1-8 suggests that there are substantial difficulties in measuring or identifying the unemployed nonwhite.

U.S. Bureau of the Census. "Estimates of the Population of Counties and Metropolitan Areas, July 1, 1966: A Summary Report," *Current Population Reports,* Series P-25, No. 427. Washington, D.C.: U.S. Government Printing Office (1969a). 86 pp.
From page 11:

> The estimates shown here are derived by giving equal weight to the results of two or three separate estimating procedures using different symptomatic data. The use of equal weights implies that the methods provide estimates of roughly comparable average accuracy. The results of tests of the separate methods are not yet conclusive enough to warrant the assignment of differential weights. A method that tends to be accurate on the average may be less accurate in a particular area.

Table H gives some idea of possible biases in the methods employed. Of the 302 metropolitan counties for which three methods were averaged to obtain the "best" estimate, the housing unit method was the highest estimate generated in over half the counties (152), but the lowest in only one sixth (50). Component Method II had the opposite tendency, being the high estimate for less than one quarter of the counties (72), but the low estimate for almost one half (147). The Composite estimate appears to have the greatest central tendency for the metropolitan counties, with 119 middle values, compared with 78 high estimates and 105 low ones.

U.S. Bureau of the Census. *Detailed Description of Selected Census Bureau Research Projects for Consideration for Fiscal Years 1971–1975, and Appropriations Requested for Fiscal Year 1970.* (1969b). 8 pp. (Unpublished.)
Project 35 (f), "Migration Package," funded for $75,000 Fiscal Year 1973, seems too small. The problems of migration appear to be the center of much of the enumeration difficulty.

Project 36 (b), "New Methods for Population Projections," sounds interesting. Does the meaning of "economic-base type projections" have something to do with econometrics? The degree of funding for this project appears reasonable, although in the long run one might desire even more than the $115,000 per annum suggested here. The funding suggested here does not seem compatible with some of the earlier and much smaller requests made for similar work.

Project 36 (c), "Population Estimates for Cities (and for Nonwhite)," and Project 36 (d), "Internal Migration and Population Trends," sound very good and very important. The high-level funding is appropriate.

Project 36 (f), "Census Evaluation: Measurement of Underenumeration," is not a very clear project. The writing is too cryptic. The specific work to be done on "geographic differentials" should be spelled out.

U.S. Bureau of the Census. *Estimates of the Population of States, July 1968 and 1969.* Current Population Reports. Series P–25, No. 436. Washington, D.C.: U.S. Government Printing Office (1970). 18 pp.
This report uses the regression method for making intercensal estimates of state populations.

U.S. Bureau of Labor Statistics. *Pilot and Experimental Program on Urban Employment Surveys.* Report No. 354. Washington, D.C. (1959). 56 pp. + unnumbered.
Chapter II discusses three relevant experiments: checking residences from lists supplied by New York City employers; checking residences from casual working-hour New York interviews; and comparing census to casual after-working-hour interviews in New Haven. It would appear that (a) techniques for matching are grossly inadequate; (b) ability to obtain information at residence for potential undercounted is grossly lacking; (c) methods of sampling to obtain meaningful results have not been proposed; and (d) because of (a)–(c), the usefulness of these techniques is doubted. Even if the difficulties are overcome, the sample sizes required to obtain precise estimates might be very large.

The information obtained led to hypotheses about the enumeration process that may well warrant further study. For important examples, see p. 2 and p. 13.

Zelnik, Melvin. "Errors in the 1960 Census Enumeration of Native Whites," *Journal of the American Statistical Association,* 59 (1964), 437–459.
Detailed analysis with major emphasis on age heaping.

Zelnik, Melvin. "An Evaluation of New Estimates of the Negro Population,"
   Demography, 2 (1965), 630–639.
Bogue, Misra, and Dandekar (1964) are criticized sharply. There is a reply by
Bogue, Misra, and Dandekar. Note top of p. 638, where it is asserted that the
nonwhite undercount occurs "primarily because of highly irregular living arrange-
ments, which characterize Negro males."

Zitter, Meyer, and Henry S. Schryock, Jr. "Accuracy and Methods of Preparing
   Postcensal Population Estimates for States and Local Areas," *Demography,* 1
   (1964), 227–241.
A survey of the various methods for making postcensal estimates by states; does
not include very much on smaller geographic areas except for those associated
with standard metropolitan areas. The results here are only for total counts. The
regression methods used here apparently do not do as well as those more closely
related to standard demographic techniques.

Zitter, Meyer, Donald E. Starsinic, and David L. Word. "Accuracy of Methods of
   Preparing Postcensal Population Estimates for Counties: A Summary Com-
   pilation of Recent Studies." Paper presented at the Population Association of
   America Meeting in Boston, April 18–20, 1968.
From pages 6 and 7:

> The pattern of deviations with respect to methods is generally similar, with Component
> Method II showing the largest deviation, followed closely by the Vital Rates method;
> and, lastly, the Composite method with considerably lower deviations. The Ratio-
> Correlation (regression) method was lowest in the two States where it was tested.
> Overall, for all areas, the average deviation for Component Method II (1,101 counties)
> was 7.5 percent; Vital Rates method (993 counties) 6.8 percent; Composite method
> (402 counties) 4.5 percent; and Ratio-Correlation method (182 counties) 4.8 percent
> (Table A). Where common methods were available (4 States, 315 counties) Component
> Method II deviation was 5.3 percent, Vital Rates method 5.4 percent, and Composite
> method 4.4 percent (Table F).
>   The evidence is very clear that lower average errors are achieved when estimates by
> different methods are averaged together. In looking at Component Method II and the
> Vital Rates method, for example, the deviation by the average of the two methods ap-
> pears to be significantly lower than that of each of the separate methods in each of the
> eleven States for which both methods were tested. The average deviation of Component
> Method II and the Vital Rates method combined in these eleven States (about 900
> counties) was 5.1 percent. An interesting anomaly is that when the Composite method,
> which represents a more sophisticated use of vital statistics for population estimation
> purposes, is substituted for the Crude Vital Rates method in the average with Method II,
> the results are not greatly improved; yet the Composite method generally yielded smaller
> deviations than the Vital Rates method in the States where both results were available.
> *The generally high average errors of the single method suggest that local estimators
> should avoid using any single method for deriving county population estimates in this
> decade.*

The data discussed are for population counts of states and counties; there is
nothing by age or sex or race.

Appendix D:
Subcommittees of the
Advisory Committee on Problems
of Census Enumeration

Subcommittee on Alternatives to the Census

I. RICHARD SAVAGE, Department of Statistics, Florida State University, Tallahassee, *Chairman*
NORMAN M. BRADBURN, Master, Social Sciences Collegiate Division, University of Chicago, Chicago, Illinois
REYNOLDS FARLEY, Population Studies Center, University of Michigan, Ann Arbor
MORRIS H. HANSEN, Senior Staff Advisor, Westat Research, Inc., Bethesda, Maryland
WILLIAM H. KRUSKAL, Department of Statistics, University of Chicago, Chicago, Illinois

Subcommittee on Alternative Instruments for Improving Census Coverage

WAYNE A. DANIELSON, Dean, School of Communication, University of Texas, Austin, *Chairman*
LIONEL BARROW, Associate Research Director, Foote, Cone & Belding, Inc., New York, New York
ARTHUR A. BUSHKIN, Information Sciences Laboratory, Lockheed Missile and Space Corporation, Palo Alto, California
REYNOLDS FARLEY, Population Studies Center, University of Michigan, Ann Arbor
ROBERT K. HOLZ, Department of Geography, University of Texas, Austin
LEON S. LIPSON, Yale Law School, New Haven, Connecticut
MAXWELL McCOMBS, School of Journalism, University of North Carolina, Chapel Hill
KARL E. TAEUBER, Department of Sociology, University of Wisconsin, Madison

Subcommittee on Data Analysis

LEO F. SCHNORE, Department of Sociology, University of Wisconsin, Madison, *Chairman*

GLEN G. CAIN, Department of Economics, University of Wisconsin, Madison

REYNOLDS FARLEY, Population Studies Center, University of Michigan, Ann Arbor

Subcommittee on Experimental Uses of the 1970 Census Public Information Campaign

WAYNE A. DANIELSON, Dean, School of Communication, University of Texas, Austin, *Chairman*

LIONEL BARROW, Associate Research Director, Foote, Cone & Belding, Inc., New York, New York

LEO BOGART, Executive Vice President and General Manager, Bureau of Advertising, American Newspaper Publishers Association, New York, New York

FRANK G. DAVIS, Chairman, Department of Economics, Lincoln University, Pennsylvania

JOHN A. DIMLING, Vice President for Research, National Association of Broadcasters, Washington, D.C.

*ROBERT B. HILL, Senior Research Staff, Bureau of Applied Social Research, Columbia University, New York, New York

Subcommittee on the Social Psychology of Anonymity I

JOHN I. KITSUSE, Department of Sociology, Northwestern University, Evanston, Illinois, *Chairman*

HOWARD S. BECKER, Department of Sociology, Northwestern University, Evanston, Illinois

ROBERT BLAUNER, Department of Sociology, University of California at Berkeley

WILLIAM H. FRIEDLAND, Department of Sociology, University of California at Santa Cruz

SHELDON L. MESSINGER, Center for the Study of Law and Society, University of California at Berkeley

DAVID SMITH, M.D., Haight-Ashbury Clinic, San Francisco, California

ANSELM L. STRAUSS, School of Nursing, University of California Medical Center, San Francisco

LENORE WEITZMAN, Department of Sociology, Columbia University, New York, New York

*Presently Deputy Director of the Research Department, National Urban League, Washington, D.C.

Subcommittee on the Social Psychology of Anonymity II

JOHN I. KITSUSE, Department of Sociology, Northwestern University, Evanston, Illinois, *Chairman*

HOWARD S. BECKER, Department of Sociology, Northwestern University, Evanston, Illinois

EGON BITTNER, Department of Sociology, Brandeis University, Waltham, Massachusetts

NORMAN M. BRADBURN, Master, Social Sciences Collegiate Division, University of Chicago, Chicago, Illinois

FRED DAVIS, Graduate Program in Sociology, University of California, San Francisco

WILLIAM H. FRIEDLAND, Department of Sociology, University of California at Santa Cruz

SHELDON L. MESSINGER, Center for the Study of Law and Society, University of California at Berkeley

ALLAN SCHNAIBERG, Department of Sociology, Northwestern University, Evanston, Illinois

JAMES SMITH, Department of Economics, Pennsylvania State University, University Park

WALTER WALLACE, Russell Sage Foundation, New York, New York

Subcommittee on Urban Ethnography

S. M. MILLER, Urban Center, New York University, New York, *Chairman*

LEONARD H. GOODMAN, Bureau of Social Science Research, Washington, D.C.

WILLIAM H. KRUSKAL, Department of Statistics, University of Chicago, Chicago, Illinois

ELLIOT LIEBOW, Center for Metropolitan Studies, National Institute of Mental Health, Rockville, Maryland

ELEANOR B. SHELDON, Russell Sage Foundation, New York, New York

Index

NOTE: "n." indicates a reference to a footnote.

D